Ruth Artmonsky

# TRADING
# TEXTILES

Fifty years of advertising for fibres and fabrics

1920–1970

Published by:
Artmonsky Arts
Flat 1, 27 Henrietta Street
London WC2E 8NA
artmonskyruth@gmail.com
Tel. 07767 820 406

Text © Ruth Artmonsky 2021

ISBN 978-1-9163845-3-8

Designed by:
David Preston Studio
www.davidprestonstudio.com

Printed in Wales by:
Gomer Press
https://gomerprinting.co.uk

My thanks to Stella Harpley and
Eduardo Sant'Anna for their help
with the images; and to Tamsin
Preston and Dr David Preston for
their enthusiasm and imaginative
book design.

# CONTENTS

Display designed by Hulme Chadwick for the British Industries Fair 1953 for ICI to invoke an 'intelligent interest' in Ardil and Terylene.

# INTRODUCTION

We feel the need exists for a concerted effort by all interested no matter in what section they may be engaged, to make the public more textile conscious … by effective publicity, directed both to the public and those who supply the public, the objective can be very largely obtained and the fullest possible measure of prosperity secured for our trade.

*Drapers' Record*, 1938

In the 1860s a young Scottish weaver, Alexander Morton, plucked up the courage to come down to London, literally walking the streets, to try to sell the wares of a local group of weavers directly to the big department stores, as Shoolbred's and Swan & Edgar. In the 1950s the textile entrepreneur Zika Ascher would watch patiently whilst Christian Dior handled all the samples Ascher had brought to him, meticulously pushing rejected ones to the left and approved ones to the right. Personal contact, whether by manufacturer, or sales agent, would always be predominant in the trading of textiles.

The selling of textiles was the last crucial step in the process from the making of the fibre, through its being woven into cloth, to its being used by the purchaser – whether the selling was to a London department store, a Paris couturier, or a housewife running up curtains or making a dress for herself at home. Press advertising was only one marketing ploy, coming late to the field, but mushrooming with the explosion of home and fashion magazines in the 1920s and '30s. In an increasingly competitive and fluctuating market textile manufacturers would come to use every means available to keep their names before the public's eye and to sell their wares.

From the time of the Great Exhibition of 1851, having ones textiles on display to the public, whether at an international, national, general or specialized exhibition, particularly where prizes were awarded, was a frequently used medium.

Warner & Sons stand at the British Empire Exhibition, 1925.

There were the regular national fairs – as the British Industries Fairs (from 1915) and the Ideal Home Exhibitions (from 1908); one-offs as the 1935 British Art & Industry Fair at Burlington House and the 1946 Britain Can Make It exhibition at the Victoria and Albert Museum; along with major overseas specialist shows, as the Milan Triennale.

The impact a display stand could have is conjured up by a Design & Industries Association report of a Women's Fair and Exhibition at the Empire Hall, Olympia in 1939:

Riette Sturge Moore arranged a very fine display of furnishing textiles in the form of a series of open stands draped with lengths of material showing fabrics by Cambell Fabrics, Courtaulds, Donald Bros., Foxton, Helios, Morton Sundour, Edinburgh Weavers, Ernest Race, Ramon Son & Crocker, Warner & Sons, and Old Bleach Linen. This display proved to be highly attractive to the general public which appeared to be surprised that such textiles existed at all…

Display feature for the Textile section at the British Industries Fair 1947, designed by Christopher Nicholson of Cockade Ltd.

Above: Viyella's Head Office. An imposing art deco building on Castle Boulevard, Nottingham, undated.

Opposite: Sanderson's showroom, Berners Street, London, undated. Designed by Slater & Uren.

And if potential buyers were in any doubt as to the quality of a textile firm's output it could display its stature, its progressiveness and how it felt it should be valued, by the buildings in which it operated, whether factory, head office or showroom. Sandersons caught on to this idea fairly early on when it commissioned Charles Voysey to design its factory at Chiswick, and then again with a rebuild of its showrooms in Berners Street, designed by Reginald Uren, which the *Architectural Review* of 1960 described as 'the world's most fabulous showrooms'. Even before the rebuild a Sanderson's exhibition mounted in Berners Street, with displays by the likes of Hugh Casson (then Professor of Interior Design at the Royal College of Art), could attract tens of thousands of visitors. From the solidness of Hollins & Sons' Viyella House in Nottingham to the glittering glass of Seker's Sloane Square showroom designed by Dennis Lennon (incidentally the first director of London's Rayon Centre), textile manufacturers hoped that potential buyers would make a natural link from the quality of its architecture to the quality of its products.

Of course when it came to making use of the press there were other ways of getting featured than

A CENTURY OF
SANDERSON

1860-1960

Sanderson have great pleasure
in inviting you to walk round
their new Showrooms and to
see the Centenary Collections
of Wallpapers and Fabrics

Opposite: Showroom for Sekers fabrics, Sloane Street, London, 1965. Designed by Brett & Pollen. Interior by Dennis Lennon.

Right: Warner & Son showroom, Wells Street (north of Oxford Street), undated.

having to compete for expensive advertising space. Whenever textiles had been chosen for a major new building or a new liner, as Tibor fabrics for the Royal Yacht Britannia, or Sundour Morton hangings for the Liverpool Philharmonic Hall, it could potentially make a news item or even a feature; and publicists would try to get pictures and accounts of launch parties for new ranges into the social columns, especially when well-known guests were in

attendance. Royal recognition, whether with assigning of Royal Warrants for firms, or knighthoods for their owners, would also provide opportunities for press releases as with the knighting of James Morton of Morton Sundour, Frank Warner and Ernest Goodale of Warner's and Miki Seker of Seker's. And then there were occasions when prizes were awarded and made noteworthy either for specific designs, as for Council of Industrial Design awards for Keith

13

# TEXTIRAMA

## INTERNATIONAL TRADE FAIR

**TEXTILES**

**CARPETS**

**FURNISHING FABRICS**

**KNITWEAR**

**CLOTHING**

**400 EXHIBITORS**

Above: Advert for one of a number of European textile exhibitions in which British manufacturers might show, *The Ambassador*, 1965.

Opposite: Liberty's typical grand window display of textiles, c. 1951.

14

Vaughan's 'Adam' for Edinburgh Weavers in 1958 and Shirley Craven's 'Le Bosquet' for Hull Traders in 1960. Or for the overall ouevre of designers as the Royal Society of Arts awarding RDI status to Allan Walton (1940) and to Lucienne Day (1962).

This book, however, focuses on the selling of textiles by the placement of advertisements in the general press, on the images and copy, and thereby, indirectly, providing a sketch of the textile industry itself, for some fifty years.

DRIVEN BY DESIGN

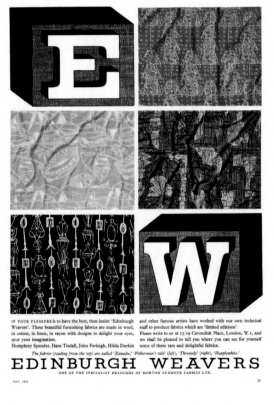

Edinburgh Weavers in full flood, *House & Garden*, 1955.

efore World War II relatively few textiles manufacturers fully appreciated the role design could play in the economics of their industry. In 1915 a group of business men and other interested parties bonded together to form the Design and Industries Association (DIA) – 'an association of manufacturers, designers, distributors, economists and critics' whose aim it was to improve the design of British manufactured products and to encourage 'a more intelligent demand amongst the public for what is best and soundest in design'. Textile manufactures did not immediately flock to join, but a few of the more progressive ones were in at the founding of DIA, or were early joiners – James Morton of Sundour Fabrics and Frank Warner, the silk manufacturer were to the fore.

It was not until 1935 that any major exhibition extolling the design, rather than the technical inventiveness, of products was mounted, when the Royal Society of Arts organized its 'Exhibition of British Art in Industry' at the Royal Academy. In preparation for this a number of advisory committees were set up of which two were for dress materials and furnishing fabrics. Their members included Samuel Courtauld, Sir Kenneth Lee of Tootal, Broadhurst,

W.H. Foxton, and E.W. Goodale of Warner's – the message was beginning to seep through.

Eventually most textile firms, some much sooner than others, began to have their own studios and employ their own designers alongside commissioning freelance ones. Several, in the 1920s and 30s dipped their toes into 'contemporary' design as the Donald Bros. with Old Glamis Fabrics using Marion Dorn and Paul Nash, and Foxton's commissioning Minnie McLeish and the noted commercial artist Gregory Brown, but then seem to have got cold feet, as it were. Lucienne Day was to complain about the situation even into the 1950s:

> One of the problems of a young designer was in fact the lack of understanding of most manufacturers as to what constituted the sort of design that one was interested in i.e. modern design.

The textile companies included in this section set out from the start to make design key, whatever the cost; and, as it was said of Edinburgh Weavers, were 'catering mainly for those seeking to establish a contemporary style'. There were some start-ups before WWII, some experiments lasting only a short time, some blossoming into profitable businesses, some becoming major players. Examples were variously run – by a textile man cum artist, Alec Walker of Crysede; by an artist from a textile family, Allen Walton of Allen Walton Textiles; and by a business man with an artist son, Tom Heron of Cresta.

Alec Walker was already alert to design when he commissioned Edward McKnight Kauffer to provide publicity for his small mill that his textile manufacturing father had given him which was producing Vigil Silk. But his enthusiasm for design took him further – to Paris to meet artists working there, which, in turn, inspired him to try his own hand at design. Settling in Newlyn he established his company, Crysede, in 1920. By 1925 he was showing his textiles in a one-man exhibition at the Independent Gallery in London. As the business grew Walker took on Tom Heron as manager, and whilst Heron transferred the production side to St Ives and began to develop a retail arm, Walker remained in his Newlyn studio creating designs. Later the two were to have a falling out, with Walker eventually turning to farming, whilst Heron set up his own company (later to purchase the remains of Crysede).

Left: A rare textile poster design by Edward McKnight Kauffer for Virgil Silk, 1919.

Above: A poster designed by Horace Taylor for Alec Walker's Virgil Silk, 1919.

ALLAN
WALTON
TEXTILES

Stocked by all leading
Retailers

Full range of new
designs by
prominent artists
on view

5o
BERNERS
STREET
LONDON : W.I
'Phone : Museum 5324/5

Director of Talks' Room
at Broadcasting House

CURTAINS OF ALLAN WALTON HAND-PRINTED
FADELESS SATIN

Advertisement showing off Allan Walton textiles
for Broadcasting House, 1934.

Allan Walton Textiles was a short-lived affair, but unique in that Walton was a trained artist (the Slade, Paris ateliers, Westminster School of Art) albeit from a textile background (his father owning a mill in Manchester). In 1931, Walton and his brother set up Allan Walton Textiles, Walton doing much of the designing himself along with commissioning some of the Bloomsbury artists, including Vanessa Bell, Duncan Grant and Frank Dobson. Walton was soon providing designs for furnishing some of the major projects of the time, as the Orient Liner Orion launched in 1934. The outstanding quality of his designed textiles was recognized when he was elected a Royal Designer of Industry by the Royal Society of Arts in 1935. Walton's firm closed at the start of WWII and he turned to academia becoming the Director of the Glasgow School of Art, his premature death later denying him the post of Professor of Design at the Royal College of Art.

But towering above these, when it came to textile firms 'driven by design' in the pre-war years, was the Edinburgh Weavers, which was to set the bar. James Morton, of Morton Sundour, decided he would like add to his more run of the mill output a line for 'persons of knowledge and good taste'; a line with its own identity, a part of Morton Sundour but apart from it. Edinburgh Weavers was originally set up in Edinburgh and consequently its name. The company took on board Edmund Hunter and his son Alec, who were struggling with their small weaving firm in Letchworth. Alec had attended the Byam Shaw School of Art, and the Hunter's first textiles for James Morton were launched in 1929. With showrooms in Hanover Square in London and selling to the likes of Liberty's and Fortnum & Mason, Edinburgh Weavers from its start marked out its patch. It was serendipity, when Alec Hunter left the company in 1931 (not wanting to relocate to Carlisle with the firm), that James had a creative son, Alastair, who was able to fill the vacancy

By 1932 Morton Sundour had established its offshoot Edinburgh Weavers with Alastair Morton as its 'styling director'. Alastair had had a kind of shortened apprenticeship through the various departments of his father's factory but was without formal art training. Niklaus Pevsner was to describe Edinburgh Weavers as a 'laboratory for the best modern textile art'. By 1935 it had set up showrooms in New Bond Street and brought in a showroom manager, Anthony Hunt, who played a

crucial role in developing contacts with the architectural and interior design markets. At this time the company startled the industry with its 'First Edition Fabrics' ('made in the modest quantities of all works of art') to be followed in 1937 by its 'Constructionist Fabrics'. From that time on Edinburgh Weavers appeared in all the major related exhibitions, sold to the most progressive retail outlets, and worked on major projects as Cunard liners and classy hotels. Besides providing designs himself, Alastair commissioned both British and European artists including Ben and Winifred Nicholson, Ashley Havinden, Marion Dorn, Doris Zinkeisen, the list goes on. Mothballed during the war, Edinburgh Weavers did not begin to operate normally again until 1949, and the 1950s and '60s were to be some of the company's most influential years.

Wartime brought a halt to design adventuring generally; but the war end brought with it a tsunami of design consciousness. The Design Council had been established in 1944 to contribute to economic recovery, declaring its aim to be 'to promote by all means the improvement of design in the products of British Industry'. Flexing its muscles early in order to validate its existence in 1946 it held an exhibition at the Victoria & Albert Museum to show off what good design was beginning to emerge from British industry – 'Britain Can Make It'. Although manufacturers were only just beginning to adjust to peace time conditions and the Utility Scheme was still in operation, Edinburgh Weavers was on display there, along with Helios and Cresta and other new boys on the textile design street.

Enid Marx writing on fabrics displayed in the exhibition bemoaned that in fact design had been neglected by:

> …manufacturers and salesmen who have been so concerned with mechanical invention and the chemical problems of dyes, that all their energies and resources have been devoted to these ends.

The objective of the Festival of Britain in 1951 was a celebration of revival not specifically aimed at encouraging 'good' design, but its immense size and varied content nevertheless gave unexpected opportunities for young textile designers to establish themselves and textile manufacturers to re-establish themselves in the public eye.

EDINBURGH WEAVERS · 102 MOUNT ST · LONDON W1

23

Rare advertisement for Helios, a subsidiary
of Barlow & Jones – Head designer Marianne
Straub, *Decorative Art*, 1940.

MIRIK (*Nuralyn*)          CHESTER (*Cotton*)          RAMSBY (*Rayon*)

HELIOS OPAQUE FABRICS
have been designed to bring
COLOUR & CHEERFULNESS
to the problems of lighting
restriction

The COLOURS are fast to
light and washing

If your Furnisher has no
stock, ask him to obtain
patterns ; or write to the
mill for the name of your
nearest retailer

HELIOS L^TD· BOLTON

London Showroom :
25-27 BERNERS ST., W.I

In 1953, *The Ambassador* magazine, the main vehicle for publicizing textiles for export, mounted its 'Painting into Textiles' exhibition at the Institute of Contemporary Art, hoping to inspire textile manufacturers to work more closely with artists thereby improving their products. Twenty five artists were commissioned for the show, and indeed the more progressive textile firms responded as desired; David Whitehead was one that purchased designs for production and thereby started a close relationship with John Piper through to 1970.

The late 1940s into the early 1950s brought a zeitgeist that design mattered, indeed might possibly be essential for economic survival. When it came to textiles, Marianne Staub was working for Helios, John Murray at David Whitehead, Patrick Heron at his father's Cresta Silks, whilst the European settlers Tibor Reich, Miki Sekers and Lida and Zika Ascher were starting up their own businesses; Terence Conran was running Conran Fabrics, Shirley Craven arrived at Hull Traders, and Isabella and Hans Tisdall had Tamesa Fabrics. Some like fireworks, burst upon the scene, showed their tricks and then burnt out, others became more firmly established.

*weaves* DEEP TEXTURES TEXTUREDRAPES TEXTUREPRINTS

TIBOR LTD., STRATFORD-ON-AVON

Most of the relatively small design-led enterprises were working for specific contracts or with small runs and rarely resorted to advertising. Typical were the Aschers, neither professionally trained as designers, both chancing their hands. Nevertheless, with supreme confidence they launched their first design range at the Dorchester Hotel with James Laver in attendance. The Aschers not only commissioned major artists, both from England and abroad, including Felix Topolski, Julian Trevelyan, Matisse, Cocteau and Calder, but showed their designs in art galleries, as Lefevre and the Redfern. Working mainly with couturier and high end retail stores as Liberty's and Harvey Nichols, they seem rarely to have advertised, one exception being a specific campaign when they tied in with ICI to produce Chemstrand.

But the leaders in the immediate post-war years were in fact three old established companies waking up to textile design – Morton Sundour with Edinburgh Weavers, David Whitehead and Heal & Son. The Whitehead group which had been founded in 1815 was reawakened when its subsidiary, formed in 1927, appointed in 1948, John Murray, an architect with no textile training, as its Director of furnishing fabrics. Although Murray was only to stay with the firm less than five years, Alan Peat in his account of the firm's history wrote of Murray's impact:

> ...the firm broke with tradition and gave the mass market gay, colourful and imaginative design…Whitehead became synonymous with the contemporary print, banishing forever the era of muddy floral and 'folksy' print fashions.

John Murray was to be remembered by his tag 'The cheap need not be cheap and nasty'!

Tom Worthington's stay at Heal's was another matter, some forty years. Although Heal's had built up a fabric department prior to the war, with Christopher Heal providing some of its designs, it was when Heal's Wholesale and Export Ltd. morphed into Heal's Fabrics, in 1948, steered by Worthington, that it became a leader when it came to design. He, and his assistant Jenni Allen, would tour every textile department in art colleges in Britain, sometimes venturing on to the Continent, in search for new young talent. In any one year they

Advertisement for David Whitehead Fabrics, not only naming designers, but also showing them, *House & Gardens*, 1953.

Advertisement for David Whitehead Fabrics, with 'cultura' sphinx drape, *House & Gardens*, 1955.

*Cretonnes designed by Christopher Heal*

## Three clever cretonnes

Imagination and intelligence at Heal's create rare and rational designs. "Granta," "Rhythm," and "A Room of One's Own" are cretonnes in witty abstract patterns for curtains and covers. Each is to be had in four or five different colour schemes.

They have a lively air, and in their crisp, clear and unfadeable colourings they will encourage any room.

**They cost 2/6 a yard and are 31″ wide.**

# HEAL'S

*Write for pattern books of cretonnes to Heal & Son, Ltd., 196 Tottenham Court Road, London, W.1.*

would see hundreds of designers and thousands of designs. Heal's major stars for the period were Lucienne Day to be followed by Barbara Brown. *The Ambassador* wrote of Heal's:

> Their vitality and modern handwriting stems directly from their forward look-ing teams of young designers and this, combined with budget prices gives them their great appeal among younger-minded people, both in this country and overseas.

The smaller design-led textile firms made relatively little use of press advertising. This could have been a matter of finance but was probably more because they tended to do short production runs for spe-cific projects when it came to furnishing fabrics or worked with couturiers when it came to fashion. Generally they were not producing for the mass market, which would inevitably have necessitated advertising. Whatever the size of design-led compa-nies, when they did resort to advertising they would tend to use publications that would be seen by design-needy clients as, in the inter-war years, DIA's *Design for To-day*, the Studio's annual *Decorative*

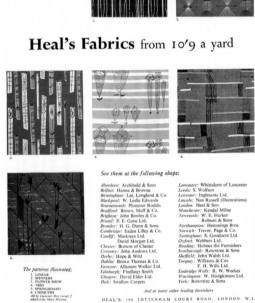

*April, 1954*

*Ideal Home*

**Heal's Fabrics** from 10'9 a yard

*See them at the following shops:*

| | |
|---|---|
| Aberdeen: Archibald & Sons | Lancaster: Whittakers of Lancaster |
| Belfast: Hanna & Browne | Leeds: S. Wolfson |
| Birmingham: Lee, Longland & Co. | Leicester: Inglesants Ltd. |
| Blackpool: W. Leslie Edwards | Lincoln: Nan Russell (Decorations) |
| Bournemouth: Plummer Roddis | London: Heal & Son |
| Bradford: Brown, Muff & Co. | Manchester: Kendal Milne |
| Brighton: John Bowles & Co. | Newcastle: W. E. Harker |
| Bristol: P. E. Gane Ltd. | Robson & Sons |
| Bromley: H. G. Dunn & Sons | Northampton: Hemmings Bros. |
| Cambridge: Eaden Lilley & Co. | Norwich: Trevor, Page & Co. |
| Cardiff: Maskreys Ltd. | Nottingham: S. Goodacre Ltd. |
| David Morgan Ltd. | Oxford: Webbers Ltd. |
| Chester: Browns of Chester | Reading: Holmes the Furnishers |
| Coventry: John Anslows Ltd. | Scarborough: Rowntree & Sons |
| Derby: Hope & Wild | Sheffield: John Walsh Ltd. |
| Dublin: Brown Thomas & Co. | Torquay: Williams & Cox |
| Eastcote: Allanson Walker Ltd. | F. H. Wills Ltd. |
| Edinburgh: Findlater Smith | Tunbridge Wells: R. W. Weekes |
| Glasgow: David Elder Ltd. | Warrington: W. Hodgkinson Ltd. |
| Hale: Swallow Carpets | York: Rowntree & Sons |

*And at many other leading furnishers*

HEAL'S, 196 TOTTENHAM COURT ROAD, LONDON. W.1.

n.33

*The patterns illustrated:*
1. LINEAR
2. SPINNERS
3. FLOWER SHOW
4. TRIO
5. SPRINGBOARD
6. CHEQUERS
*All by Lucienne Day except 2
which is by Mary Warren*

*Art* and the various architectural monthlies. When it came to more general magazines *Ideal Home* appears to have been the favoured one, at least in the inter-war years.

An advertising feature that tended to distinguish design-led textile companies from the more run-of-the-mill ones, was their preparedness to include the names of the designers of the textiles being advertised; even such a relatively small firm as Tibor Fabrics, whose owner did much of its designs would add the name of a commissioned designer when one had been used. With Heal's it became customary in their press advertising to always include the designer's name, examples being, in the 1950s, along with Lucienne Day, those of Paule Vezelay and Michael O'Connor, into the '60s Barbara Brown, Howard Carter and Peter Hall. David Whitehead even went so far as, in a 1953 advertisement, to include photos of the designers themselves (Terence Conran and Jacqueline Groag).

Several of the design-led companies provided, on their advertisements, lists of retail outlets from which their products could be purchased. This not only gave out useful information but indicated that purchase could only be made at the most

29

Heal's advertising Howard Carter's
'Pansies' and Barbara Brown's
'Recurrence', *The Ambassador*, 1963.

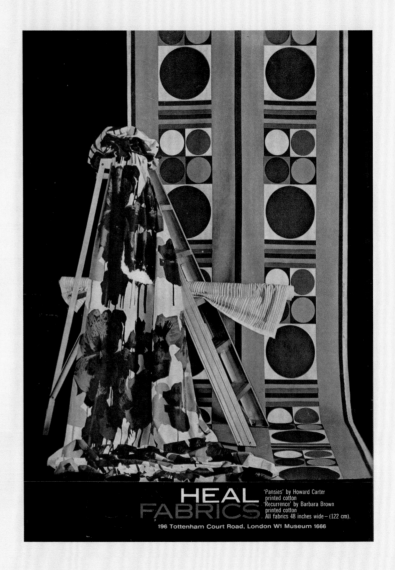

design-conscious shops and stores of that area, as in London and its suburbs, the likes of Heal's itself (which also sold Edinburgh Weavers textiles), Primavera, Peter Jones and Dunn's of Bromley; and beyond London, Kendal Milne in Manchester, David Morgan in Cardiff and Harvey Nichols in Bournemouth. David Whitehead, aiming at a wider market included more modest venues as Blackpool, Coventry and Plymouth. As naming the designer would make the reader aware of who was who in the textile world of the day, so naming outlets would provide the reader with an idea of the more risk-taking operators when it came to the retail selling the more progressive designs.

Although many of this group of companies had early advertisements with copy providing basic details as to widths, colour ranges etc., with increasing confidence, if not swagger, the offerings came to consist largely of swathes of material, nearly completely covering the space, merely accompanied by the name and logo of the company. Occasionally the fabric would be draped around a 'cultural' object, as a sphinx, to emphasise its classiness, a preferred style of David Whitehead; although Heal's resorting to a tiger cub is not so clear a link.

Generally these companies were as design conscious in their advertising as they were in their textile production. Even Liberty's which advertised rarely, with pre-war dull showings of some old eastern tapestry, in the 1940s turned to one of the leading graphic designers of the time – Ashley Havinden of Crawford's advertising agency – who devised lively, simple advertisements, and even posters, a rarity in textile advertising at that time.

No. 4463 — Volume 165       The Illustrated London News. November 1. 1924.

**ZINOVIEFF—AND THE ELECTION.**

# THE ILLUSTRATED
# LONDON NEWS
1/-

**FOR DRESSES AND JUMPERS**

**FOR CHILDREN'S FROCKS & COATS**

# LIBERTY
# VELVETEEN
## PATTERN BOOKS OF THE
## NEW COLOURINGS FOR THE AUTUMN SEASON POST FREE
10/6 A YARD. 26 INS, WIDE. 12/9 A YARD. 35 INS, WIDE. LIBERTY & CO. LTD REGENT ST. W. I

Rare Liberty's textile advertisement,
*The Illustrated London News,* 1924.

Liberty 'Fast Colour Printed Linens'
advertisement, *Ideal Home*, 1936.

Crawford's rebranding of Liberty,
by Ashley Havinden, 1948–1951.

DRIVEN BY SCIENCE

The textile industry, broadly, has a history of veering towards caution rather than taking risks. The coming of man-made fibres to revolutionise the textile industry can be fairly ascribed to industrial chemists rather than textile manufacturers, although there is the odd example of an initiative from inside the industry before the onslaught from outsiders. ICI, in one of its publicity campaigns, unearthed such a one. John Mercer, a mere bobbin winder, who, in 1844, investigated the action of caustic soda on cotton and began to experiment with cellulose; self-taught, when it came to chemistry, his experiments in dyeing, printing and finishing helped him to a management level and led ICI to brand him 'the father of textile chemistry'.

Fast forward, towards the end of the nineteenth century, another 'amateur' chemist, apprenticed in a textile mill, but, in this instance, the mill of his father, Alexander Morton, was James Morton. Folklore has it that James, on one of his selling expeditions to London, spied some of the company's fabrics draped in a Liberty's shop window, faded due to exposure to the sun. True or not, James began to explore the chemistry of dyeing in order to achieve a great fastness of colour, whether the company's fabrics were going to be exposed to sunlight or washing. Searching for suitable chemists to help him, and experimenting for over a year, by 1904 Liberty's was advertising its tapestries in 'new permanent colours'. James realized the need for campaigns to persuade the conservative trade to accept his new dyes and advertisements began to appear in such magazines as *Country Life* and *The Queen*. The fabrics introducing the new dyes were brand named Sundour – the company Alexander Morton & Co. morphed into Morton Sundour Fabrics in 1914.

It was said that by the early 1920s no textile firm at the time employed so many academic chemists as Morton Sundour; James, himself, became a member of the government's 'Dyestuff Industry Development Committee' and, in 1925, the first recipient of the Faraday Medal:

> …in recognition of the signal service he has rendered to chemical science and industry during the last ten years.

Steadfast Dyes and Printers, set up by James, not only served its parent company, but the trade in general.

*Aspects of an Industry*

SORCERY

THE sorcerer was reputed to have the power of converting human beings into strange animals. He turned princesses into frogs — men into swine. As the change was almost always for the worst, his magic powers were greatly feared — and with good reason! The sorcerer of the present day is the organic chemist, but his work is everywhere welcomed, because the changes he makes possible are always for the better. Have you ever seen a piece of cotton cloth coming straight from the loom ? A drab and shabby-looking article indeed. But see it later, after it has been cleaned, softened, filled, made creaseless and given a lustre. What a transformation is there . . . sow's ear into silk purse, toad into princess . . . a transformation directly due to the wide range of textile chemicals known as auxiliary products, made by the British dyestuffs industry. There is little that the British organic chemists cannot do with textiles. They have auxiliary products which make cotton as transparent as glass, others which soften it to resemble swansdown or make it so stiff that a pleated collar sticks out like an old-time ruff. They can make cotton look like silk or dull the lustre of rayon. They have chemicals known as stripping agents, which take the dye out of a fabric, and wetting agents, which make materials more absorbent. They have even evolved a product which enables the softest fabric to repel water without loss of texture. It is no exaggeration to say that the chemist through these organic auxiliary products *makes* the modern fabric. It is the chemist who transforms it from a lifeless material into the highly attractive, beautifully finished product you buy in the shops.

*Imperial Chemical Industries Ltd., London, S.W.1*

Sundour was not only unique in its break-through for 'fast dyes', but in the style, and indeed, onslaught, of its advertising and the role it gave to its advertising designer Charles Paine. The company not only used Paine for its advertising but drew him in to design for its textiles as well. Sundour employed Charles Hobsons, the distinguished Manchester agency, for its advertising, its copy being written by w. Haslam Mills, leader writer of the *Manchester Guardian*. Textiles had never before seen such advertisements. One example, showing a standard bearer in the army, carried the copy:

He is serving with the Colours. He carries the Colours. It is a point of honour with him that the Colours should never be lost. So it is with Sundour fabrics. Every Sundour fabric serves with its colours. No Sundour fabric ever fades. Sun-fast and wash-fast.

Charles Paine was later to work for the Baynard Press, its director, Fred Philips, then being brought in to undertake Morton Sundour's advertising. And through to the 1930s and '40s major designers as

36

-with his coat so gay

# SUNDOUR
## UNFADABLE FABRICS

Sundour Unfadable Fabrics advertisement, designed by Charles Paine, 1929.

Ashley Havinden and Hugh Casson were commissioned to work on Sundour advertisements. The message remained the same from the 1920s in *Ideal Home*:

> Will save you from all anxiety as to fading, even when exposed to the strongest sunshine which only serves to reveal their beauty of colour.

To the same magazine in 1954:

> So insist on Sundour. Sundour fabrics are guaranteed against fading – most of them for the whole of their life.

Susannah Handley, writing on the development of man-made fibres, accredited two émigré French families with this revolution of the textile industry – the Courtaulds and the Du Ponts. Although Courtauld is usually thought to have made the breakthrough when it turned from its previous success in making silk crepe for Victorian mourning to becoming the biggest manufacturer of rayon, it could not have done this without developments in the chemical industry.

★ SOFA GAIETY ★

Oh fie for shame,
You naughty chairs,
The sun has found you out!
Your covers worn,
The colours dimmed
Put all your grace to rout.

You lazy things
Now rouse yourselves!
Don't just sit there and glower!
Come let me choose
You gayer clothes
Of my beloved Sundour.

**Sundour**
FURNISHING **fabrics**

TAPESTRIES · BROCADES · VELVETS · CRETONNES
FOR CASEMENTS, CURTAINS AND COVERS · CAN BE
OBTAINED FROM ALL GOOD FURNISHING HOUSES

GUARANTEED UNFADABLE by *Morton Sundour Fabrics Limited, Carlisle*

*People know more about furnishings than they did. They know
that besides convenience, a room needs that extra touch of life
which makes it good to live in, and which depends so much on
fabrics wisely chosen. This is what the public have come to
think of when they hear the name of Sundour fabrics.*

**Sundour**
FINE FURNISHING FABRICS

MORTON SUNDOUR FABRICS LTD. 15-19 CAVENDISH PLACE LONDON W1 DENTONHILL WORKS CARLISLE ENGLAND
T10

Sundour advertisement with 'unfadable' still
the focus, *Woman's Journal*, 1935.

Sundour 'Fine Furnishing Fabrics' advertisement,
illustrated by Hugh Casson, 1946.

From the end of the nineteenth century the French had been experimenting with the use of cellulose for making artificial silk. Working with the same basic product, but within the paper rather than the textile industry, a trio of English chemists had been working with wood pulp, naming the resulting product 'viscose'. C.E. Cross, one of the three, took out a patent for this, and with a partner set up a company, which, in 1902, became the Viscose Development Company making lamp filaments and artificial silk. Courtaulds, with the market for mourning silk in decline, was, at the time, looking for alternatives. Its director, Henry Tetley, set his sights on viscose. In spite of the reluctance of his fellow directors who, he declared, knew nothing about chemistry, he won the day. Courtaulds brought up Cross's patents and was transformed, as Susan Handley put it, 'from a textile firm into a chemical firm with a textile branch'. Rayon, the market name for artificial silk, the viscose fibre, was launched on the British market, and Courtaulds came to dominate rayon production worldwide.

In the 1920s Courtaulds advertised its artificial silks under various brand names – Luvisca, and

Advertisement publicising Courtalds' range of fibres, *Ideal Home*, 1930.

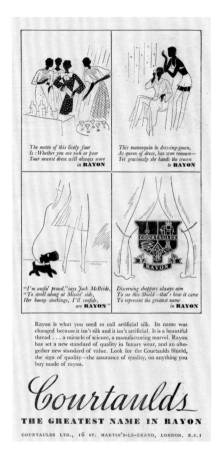

Above: Courtalds resorting to the generic term 'rayon', *Miss Modern*, 1936.

Right: Courtalds advertisement for rayon, *Vogue*, 1952.

40

Delysia – using such hype as 'imbued with the glory of the finest silk'. By the 1930s Courtaulds was taking full pages for its advertisements so as to list all its variously named rayon yarns, adding to Luvisca and Delysia, Courgette, San-Toy, Clytic, Courcain, Viscaline and Xantha. Eventually the company seems to have come to the conclusion that simplification was what the market needed and just used 'rayon' as a generic term, adding 'Courtaulds, the greatest name in rayon'. A typical advertisement appearing in *Miss Modern* in 1936 assured the public:

> Rayon is what you used to call artificial silk,
> Its name changed because it isn't silk and
> it isn't artificial. It's a beautiful thread – a
> miracle of science, a manufacturing marvel.

Just before WWII Courtaulds seems to have lapsed back into introducing a brand name – Viscana – but advertising it with the same advantages it had ascribed to rayon:

> …easy to wash, to iron, to wear, keeps its
> shape, keeps its colour, lasts very long, costs
> very little.

Courtalds returns to brand naming fibres, with 'Viscana', *Woman's Journal*, 1952.

Below: Courtalds brings brand-naming to furnishing fabric, with 'Duracour', *House & Garden*, 1960.

Right: Courtalds plugs fashion, with Springtime Tweeds from 'Courtelle', *The Ambassador*, 1963.

**NEW RICH TEXTURES . . .**

**NEW BRILLIANT COLOURS . . .**

**NEW GAY PRINTS . . .**

**Chair by Minty**
Duracour's *child-proof!* Even sticky finger-marks disappear with a damp cloth.

# and they all sponge clean!

Easy-care elegance for every home with Duracour, the luxury-weave furnishing fabric. Fade-proof, moth-proof Duracour resists dust, dirt and water, too, which means most spills—even ink!—mop off without trace. It's easy to sew, tack or stick, and can't stretch or fray. So you can furnish your home in luxurious textures and bright colours and forget cleaning worries. Duracour always stays as fresh as new with a damp cloth!

New designs, new colours, new textures. You can choose from a wealth of wonderful colours and deep, rich textures, at a price as practical as the fabric itself. There are new tweed-inspired fabrics, soft and warm to the touch, yet as strong and hard-wearing as they're beautiful. There are plain weaves in rich colours, or gay new prints in modern and traditional designs. You'd never guess such luxurious fabrics are made to sponge clean!

**HOW TO GET DURACOUR**

Leading furniture manufacturers use Duracour, and you can buy it by the yard (48" wide) for upholstery, and a hundred-and-one home uses. Look at the Duracour pattern book in any good store. If you have any difficulty in obtaining what you need, write to : Courlak Limited, 143 New Bond Street, London, W.1.

A COURTAULDS PRODUCT

# DURACOUR
### the fabric you just sponge clean

HOUSE & GARDEN

*Below* **Marcel Fenez** styled this Courtelle and wool woven tweed dress and it's sheer feminine flattery! It's beautifully modelled. Pleated perfectly—permanently. *Style 7670. Sizes 10-16. In pink, lime green and yellow.*

*Right* **Polly Peck** Courtelle and wool lightweight woven tweed dress. It's got a long lean line and a Ben Casey collar and quite simply, it's perfect. *Style No. 1741. Sizes 10-14. Pink/green and blue/yellow.*

*Extreme Right* **Linzi** Courtelle and wool tweed coat dress—the smartest cover story for almost anything this Spring. *Style 'Blenheim' in Sizes 10-18 Black/white, brown/white and blue/white mixtures.*

# Courtelle's
## Springtime Tweeds

Tweeds, tweeds, Spring-into-Summer tweeds. Woven with traditional skill—in the fibre that's strictly for moderns! Shown here are only three translations of Courtelle/wool tweed, but you can see how fashion loves it!

*For enquiries contact the Courtelle marketing offices in :—*
*London, Copenhagen, Stockholm, Amsterdam, Paris, New York and Sydney Courtelle, Courtaulds Limited, 22 Hanover Square, London, W.1.*

COURTELLE*
* Regd. trademark for Courtaulds acrylic fibre

TCE 585

With Duracour, Courtaulds brought such easy care to furnishings:

> Fade-proof, moth-proof Duracour resists
> dust, dirt and water too, which means most
> spills – even ink! – mop off without a trace.
> It's easy to sew, tack or stick, and can't
> stretch or fray.

And similarly when marketing Courtelle – no fraying, no scuffing, no going into holes.

Next came Nylon – a completely man-made fibre. Whilst the Huguenot Courtaulds were settling in England, to eventually become masters of the semi-synthetic rayon, the Du Ponts, French chemists, emigrated to America, initially coming to dominate the market for explosives. Partially ashamed of their image as manufacturers of lethal products, and after many years of chemical and engineering research, Du Pont gave birth to 'nylon', a name they were never to trade mark, but one that was quickly taken up throughout the international textile industry. Whereas Courtaulds had merely adopted rayon for its similarity to silk, Du Pont broke entirely new ground producing fibres based on petro-chemicals.

Nylon came to England via a Du Pont licence to ICI, a company already linked to the textile industry, providing chemicals for dyestuffs, bleaches and the like. In addition ICI obtained the world rights to the polyester that the chemists of the Calico Printers Association had developed in the early years of the second world war. With such a base ICI built up a separate division devoted to fibre production, which as ICI Fibres became the biggest synthetic fibre producer in Europe. Although held back in its development of nylon during the war, ICI nevertheless, in its wartime advertising, was determined to keep its name before the public. A 1944 advertisement placed the chemist at the centre of its new product:

> …at the moment nylon is playing its part in
> the national effort and will not be available
> to the public until the war is over… The
> modern girl has good reason to be grateful
> to the chemist who has brought soft and
> beautiful fabrics within the reach of all.

And it was the 'modern' girl ICI was to target in its publicity and advertising, persuading young

ICI Fibres Division + British Nylon Spinners = ICI FIBRES LIMITED

**the new giant of synthetic fibres in Europe**

The association, on 1st January, 1965, of ICI Fibres Division with British Nylon Spinners Limited, to form the largest single concern producing synthetic fibres in Europe, is a landmark in the history of the British textile industry. The new company will have hitherto unequalled resources for research and development, and the benefit to the industry as a whole will be considerable. Through increasingly constructive co-operation with the industry in the future, ICI Fibres Limited hope to help it continue to be the most successful, adaptable and inventive textile industry in the world.

'BRI-NYLON' 'CRIMPLENE' 'TERYLENE' 'ULSTRON'

designers and boutique owners, as Marion Foale and Sally Tuffin, Mary Quant and John Stephen, to experiment with its new petro-chemical fibres resulting in an explosion of colour along the Kings Road and Carnaby Street.

Terylene, one of ICI's polyester fibres, launched in 1946, was to be used in furnishings as well as fashion. A 1958 advertisement in *House & Gardens* listed its many household uses and advantages:

> You can get tablecloths, brocade curtains, upholstery, pillows and pillow cases, quilts, blankets and sheets, all with the advantages you have come to expect from 'Terylene'; all with lightness, strength, long wear, and the wonderful talent for never stretching or shrinking.

Although developed in the 1940s Terylene does not seem to have been intensively marketed until the 1950s as an article on it in *Art & Industry* in 1953 refers to it as 'new'. It was shown at the British Industries Fair of that year and was being hyped as:

It's
Cresta
with
Ascher
and

'TERYLENE'
*Polyester* ICI *Fibre*

Cresta Couture take
Ascher's 'Terylene'/cotton,
exotically printed in
a design of Peking roses,
and produce an uncluttered
sheath dress in the new
loose-top idiom, swathed with
luxurious, matching taffeta.
Choose it in lacquer pink
or pagoda blue on
tobacco-brown leaves.

*Sizes 10-16. Price 12½ gns.*
*Cresta 152 New Bond Street, London, W.1.*
*and at all Cresta branches*

*'Terylene' is the trademark*
*for the polyester fibre made by*
IMPERIAL CHEMICAL INDUSTRIES
LIMITED, LONDON

TE 565

Left: ICI, Cresta and Ascher's shared
advertisement for 'Terylene' Polyester Fibre,
*The Queen*, 1960.

Above: Advertisement for 'Crimplene',
a derivative of Terylene, *Vogue*, 1967.

...not a mere substitute for existing natural fibres but filaments which could be spun into yarn and woven into cloth which exhibits properties and characteristics very different from those found in other material.

Although Terylene was widely advertised for household textiles, ICI quickly set out to court the fashion world with it, and its derived fibre Crimplene, used for jersey fabrics. Some twenty leading dress manufacturers were persuaded to produce clothing using the products and soon *The Ambassador* was putting out:

> While spiders attend to their own needs
> ICI meets the need of fashion and industry.
> With Terylene – the most widely promoted
> Polyester in the world.

A 1960s advertisement in *The Queen* shows how ICI was able to ride on the backs of manufacturers and retailers to market its products – it displayed a dress made by Cresta from Ascher produced Terylene cotton, the Terylene trademark standing clear from the copy with the explanation:

Advertisement for British Nylon Spinners, *Modern Woman*, 1949.

'Terylene' is the trademark for the polyester fibre made by the Imperial Chemical Industries Ltd.

All three companies (ICI, Cresta and Ascher) benefited from the one advertisement. ICI continued with other supplies to the textile industry. Well advertised from the 1960s was Procion, a range of dyes also linked to fashion:

> The tremendous shade range of PROCION dyes ensures the visual excitement and impact demanded in up-to-the-minute fashion fabrics.

Besides developing its own fibres, ICI had a period when it chummed up with Courtaulds to set up a company specifically to push nylon – British Nylon Spinners (BNS), established in 1958. If each of the parent companies was investing a goodly budget in advertising its own products, this seemed dwarfed for a time by the bombardment in the press for BNS's branded Bri-Nylon, its unique selling points listed repeatedly:

> No trouble washing it
> No time drying it
> No need to iron it
> Nothing to mend
> No perspiration clues
> No sign of wearing thin

Eventually there was a falling out and ICI was to buy up Courtaulds share in BNS, the acquisition turning the ICI Fibres Division into ICI Fibres Ltd.

A further science led enterprise drawn into textiles was British Celanese. During WWI the British government had brought two brothers over from Switzerland where they had been working on cellulose acetate, thought useful for aircraft construction. After the war, in 1923, the company was registered as British Celanese (a combination of the words 'cellulose' and 'ease'). The company retained Osborne Royds as its advertising agency, and by the late 1920s advertisements began to appear extolling a new yarn 'Cellanese':

> For beauty only the costliest silk-and-wool mixture can compare with Celanese; for wear and washing nothing is its equal.

Below: Advertisement for Celanese,
produced by Osborne Royds and Company,
*Commercial Art*, 1929.

Right: ICI advertisement for its range of
fibres, *Ark*, 1969.

Made from the finest wool, reinforced
with the soft strength of 'Celanese' yarn,
these dainty garments will wash and
wear splendidly without shrinking losing
nothing of their lovely caressing softness
through the hardest wear.

In 1957, British Celanese was absorbed by
Courtaulds, intent, as it was, on extending its ranges. It was British Celanese, within the Courtauld
group, that was to produce Tricel, marketing the
product widely, both nationally and internationally.
By the early 1960s Tricel was well established, its
advertising trumpeting its qualities – easy to wash,
rapid to dry, requiring little or no ironing, not
prone to shrink or stretch, and soil and stain resis-
tant. Tricel became a versatile player in the fashion
industry as suggested in a 1964 advertisement in
*The Ambassador*:

Whether fashion favours the look of silk,
the look of linen, the tailored look of
tweed, or the sleek look of jersey – Tricel
can make the fabrics.

Synthetic fibres became part of everyday life, in
what people wore and in their furnishings. Handley
aptly describes the transformation of the industry:

…a three-part drama between the research
chemist, the fibre textile manufacturer and
the consumer, scripted by the advertising
agencies.

The advertisements of science led fibre and fabric
manufacturers largely extolled the physical qualities
of their products – durability and ease of handling –
aesthetics rarely intruded.

# FURNISHING TRADITIONALISTS

Although textile manufacturers, in the period covered here, had, at various times, produced both for the home furnishing and the clothing markets, the tendency was towards a commitment to one or the other. Horrockses started with its feet in both camps but was to become a major player in the fashion world. Grafton's, known for its furnishing fabrics, seems to have had a short-lived venture into selling fashion with its anti-shrink fabrics. Only the scientifically led giants of synthetic fibres – Courtaulds and ICI – actively advertised their products across the whole textile market.

The manufacturers, grouped together in this section, were not particularly scientifically driven, yet, once others had built up a market with novel fibres and fabrics, would adopt the then proven products; and although some might have dipped their toes into risky 'contemporary' design, they were not fully committed in that direction either. The likes of Donald Bros., The Old Bleach Linen Company, and Foxton's, all seem to have joined the art deco band-wagon in the 1920s and '30s, at least for brief periods, before returning to familiar safe markets. Foxton's in the 1920s made use of such progressive designers as Minnie McLeish and

Below: Traditionalists Old Glamis dipping their toe into modernism, *Architectural Review*, 1934.

Below: Warner, another traditionalist, with their own attempt at modern advertising, *Design for To-day*, 1934.

# OLD GLAMIS FABRICS

For generations the firm of Donald Bros. has carried on a tradition of honest craftsmanship. Old Glamis furnishing fabrics are to-day known and used all over the world.

**DONALD Bros., Ltd.** *London Showrooms :*
D U N D E E    287, Regent Street, W.1

The Sign of Fine Design.

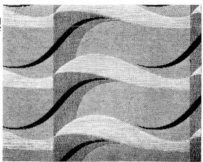

The "Mendip" Tapestry (Regd. Design).

Warner Fabrics comprise hand and power, woven and printed materials of all kinds for hangings and upholstery, ranging from facsimile reproductions of the glories of the past to the latest conceptions of contemporary design.

# WARNER FABRICS

FROM ALL LEADING DECORATORS
**WARNER & SONS LTD.**
10-13 NEWGATE STREET, LONDON, E.C.1
Factories : Braintree, Essex, and Dartford, Kent.

CVS - 22

Gregory Brown, as has been noted. Even the most traditional of furnishing fabric manufacturers, Turnbull and Stockton, with its mainly floral offerings, branded as Rosebank, seems to have had some temptation towards the geometric of that time. However, none of the companies in this section would, nowadays, be in the first to come to mind as being progressively design-led.

Even Warner's, who had taken on Alec Hunter when he resigned from Edinburgh Weavers, and had adopted Marianne Straub, when it took over Helios, remained firmly tied to the establishment. Originally the company had been quite 'earthy', its founder, Benjamin, a Jacquard engineer, manufacturing weavers' harnesses. But by the late nineteenth century Warner & Sons were manufacturing furnishing silks, and taking its designs from old records and samples in the Victoria and Albert Museum; whilst Frank Warner spent much of his time courting the great and the good, having the company's focus on palaces, embassies and country mansions, and the ilk. Although Frank's son-in-law, E.W. Goodale did make some attempt to broaden Warner's appeal socially, well into the 1960s it was still advertising such textiles as 'Pavilion', a printed cotton designed

Traditionalists Old Bleach with their attempt at modernism, *Homes & Gardens*, 1936.

An advertisement for Turnbull Stockdale's Rosebank brand, *Woman's Journal*, 1937.

Warner Fabrics publicity at its most traditional, *The Ambassador*, 1962.

from a xv century Persian miniature, and its Leisure Hour Range featured hunting, shooting, sailing, pheasants, clipper ships and gambling! However many of these traditional companies, with the bulk of their outputs safely conventional, would nevertheless try to present themselves in their advertising as having a foot in both camps. Warner's, in its 1930s advertisements described its fabrics as:

> ...ranging from facsimile reproductions of the glories of the past to the latest conceptions of contemporary design.

And, in the post-war years Rosebank was claiming in its 1960s advertising:

> ...tradition or modern, you will find just what you want in the latest Rosebank range of furnishing fabrics.

*The Ambassador* magazine referred to the Rosebank range as 'new designs in the English tradition'. When Ivon Sanderson took over the helm of his grandfather's company he similarly hedged his bets giving his objectives as:

> To provide quality merchandise as pure in tradition and period pattern as it is up to date in modern design.

Foxton's, whilst in the 1950s advertising such as 'a glazed chintz finely engraved in the Toile de Jouy style', nevertheless added:

> W. Foxton Ltd., pioneers in the contemporary style in Furnishing Fabrics, also produces of the best period effects.

By their advertising one can infer the characteristics of the firms themselves. This was evident when Warner's decided to place an advertisement in the Royal College of Art student magazine *Ark* in the same issue as a David Whitehead advertisement – showing a stark contrast between the stuffiness of the former and the jazzy eye-catching copy and layout of the latter.

Advertisements for these traditional furnishing fabric manufacturers were usually of a standard half or quarter page space. The Old Bleach Company did venture into full-page advertising in the 1940s, but it was Sanderson who took the lead with full pages

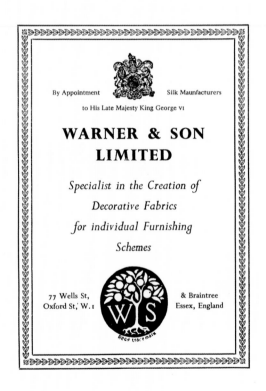

By Appointment     Silk Maunfacturers

to His Late Majesty King George VI

# WARNER & SON LIMITED

*Specialist in the Creation of*

*Decorative Fabrics*

*for individual Furnishing*

*Schemes*

77 Wells St,         & Braintree
Oxford St, W.1      Essex, England

regularly in the 1950s and '60s. Sanderson had built its reputation on its wallpapers, initially importing designs from the Continent before beginning to produce its own. It had started manufacturing fabrics as early as the immediate post-WW1 years, building a special factory for the purpose at Uxbridge. But it was a third generation Sanderson, Ivon, who was to build up its fabrics side, travelling all over the world to do so. It is possible that its full-page advertisements were in response to those of David Whitehead's as they resembled them in layout, but perhaps never quite matched them. Most frequently the Sanderson's advertisements would include both wallpapers and fabrics, killing the two birds with one stone. From current standards the match between the two was not always well-considered, and it was only in 1960 that Sanderson brought out its first range of specifically co-ordinated design.

By the 1950s the fabric side had grown sufficiently in popularity to stand on its own in advertisements, and, as with Whitehead's, the cloth was shown draped with an object – an antique chair or a violin. There appears to have been a short period when Sanderson's tried to appeal more personally to the public by introducing 'our man' not

*Terence Conran, Roger Nicholson and Marion Mahler are only a few of the contemporary artists who through the medium of David Whitehead Fabrics have been able to bring a new freedom of expression to textile design and a new approach to the art of furnishing. David Whitehead Fabrics have in themselves immeasurably widened the appeal of contemporary design in the home.*

# DAVID WHITEHEAD FABRICS

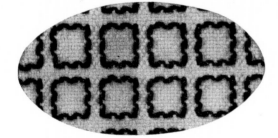

*D. Whitehead Ltd., Higher Mill, Rawtenstall, Lancs.*

ONE OF THE DAVID WHITEHEAD GROUP

KNOWLES

57

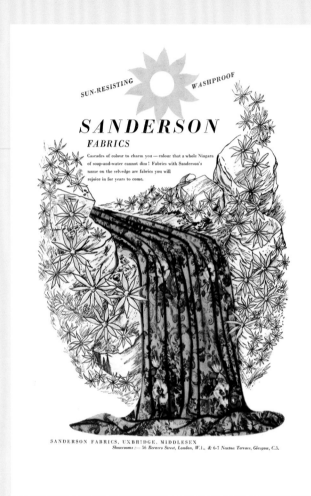

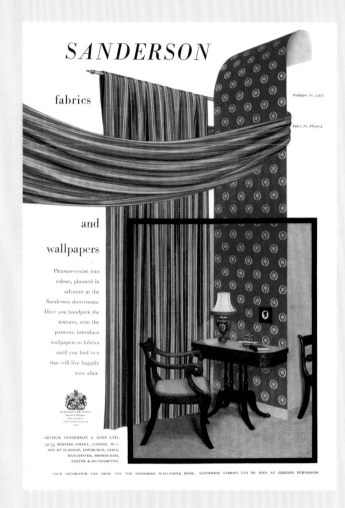

Sanderson Fabrics stand on their own, 'Sun-resisting' and 'Washproof', *Woman's Journal*, 1952.

Sanderson Fabrics initially advertised with wallpapers, *House & Garden*, 1958.

unlike the wise and successful Mr Barrett advertising shoes – 'This is one of our man's more recent finds' and so on, but the copy reads awkwardly and the idea seems to have been soon dropped.

Early advertisements for furnishing fabrics from the different firms tended to contain similar information – the type of fabric, its dimensions, the colour range available, where and how it could be used, its cost, and where it could be seen and obtained. Typical were Turnball and Stockdale's Rosebank advertisements:

> No. 9281 A 31" faceless cotton at 2/6 a yard, in black and green. Also in shades of green and brown – orange and brown – blue.

> Go to your shop today. Browse over Rosebank Pattern Books that you'll see there. Handle the Rosebank Fabrics actually in stock.

Throughout the inter-war years the potential customer was being advised to write in for further information if problems were experienced, for lists of local retailers carrying the stock, for illustrated booklets, and for samples. Into the 1950s Rosebank advertisements offered these:

> How much easier to be able to try out actual samples of furnishing fabrics in your own home, against your furniture and wall colours.

Advertisements were used to suggest every which way customers could know about, see, and handle the furnishing textiles being produced. Sanderson's, of course, used the magnet of its fine new showroom in Berner Street:

> Here you handpick the textures, scan the patterns, introduce wallpaper to fabrics, until you find two that will live happy ever after.

When it came to selling points made in the copy of the advertising of furnishing textiles, the obvious ones were durability, non-fading, non-shrinking, and ease of cleaning. Typical was The Old Bleach Linen Company in the 1930s assuring its potential

A sample advertisement from Sanderson's short-lived 'Our Man' series, *Home*, 1961.

buyers that its fabrics were:

> …woven in flax, slow to soil and hard-wearing, in colours that are beautiful and fast.

Grafton's, in its advertising in the 1950s and '60s made much of non-shrinking as well as non-stretching:

> Goodbye to ugly gaps between sill and curtain after washing! Goodbye to too loose covers! No more saggy-baggy curtains or covers either!

In one *Home & Garden* offering from 1958, Grafton let the words 'NON-SHRINK' stand larger than life, actually dwarfing the manufacturer's own name, so important did it consider this quality as a selling point.

Although the previous example contained a number of exclamation marks, furnishing fabric advertisements, in the period being considered, generally avoided strident hype, but by that perhaps could be said to have had less of the marketing energy to be found in the then contemporary advertising

Only things most exquisite of
their kind were represented
in the Queen's Doll's House.
All the linen was Old Bleach

The Linen Room       The Queen's Doll's House

## 'Old Bleach' in exquisite miniature

A DAMASK Tablecloth, perfect in miniature—minute d'oyleys and fairy-fine runners — infinitesimal sheets and towels—the perfection of Old Bleach Linen is concentrated in these tiny things.

There are Old Bleach Linens of every texture ; rich, smooth linens for sheets and pillowcases, fine lawns for embroidery, snowy damasks and soft huckabacks.

The beauty of Old Bleach is in the fabric itself. It owes nothing to chemicals or 'dressings.' It is woven from pure Irish flax and bleached by the old tried ways of sun and grass. That is why its lovely lustre survives laundering. Old Bleach Linen is

woven not only for Queens' Dolls' Houses and Queens' Palaces, but to bring beauty and good service into your own home.

*A Note on Needlework*

If you are interested in fine needlework, you should consult "The Embroideress"— the most fascinating periodical published on the subject.

You can buy "The Embroideress" at all good needlework shops or direct from the Old Bleach Linen Company. Single copies are 1/2 post free ; the annual subscription, also post free, is 4/8. Old Bleach Linens are stocked everywhere that good linens are sold ; or your nearest agent's address can be obtained from :—

*A tablecloth, d'oyleys & traycloths in the Queen's Doll's House*

## THE OLD BLEACH LINEN CO LTD
*Randalstown Northern Ireland.*

# Sunflowers at Sea

Stimulating pattern and colour give a new air to the redecorated Long Gallery of the Union-Castle liner, *Pretoria Castle*. The scheme is built round the colourings of the Old Glamis printed linen, SUNFLOWERS, used for the curtains. The grey, emerald, apple, canary, and chocolate of this pattern are echoed in the Old Glamis heavy weaves, WHITHORN, IONA and MALVERN which cover the chairs and settees and in the DON QUIXOTE cotton damask used on the high-backed settles. This is a splendid example of the general trend to the lighter and brighter treatment of public rooms.

Architects, interior designers and buyers are welcome visitors to our London or Dundee showrooms. Here we can show you Old Glamis furnishing fabrics which cannot be seen elsewhere; a range prepared exclusively for contract work; designs which can be produced in colours to suit your schemes. Look in, if you can, or write to us about your problems. We will gladly give you the address of your nearest Old Glamis stockist.

THE OLD GLAMIS HOME-MAKER'S COLOUR GUIDE provides a new and ingenious way of planning colour schemes. Let us know if you would like a free copy posted to you.

BY APPOINTMENT MAKERS OF
OLD GLAMIS FURNISHING AND EMBROIDERY FABRICS
TO H.M. QUEEN ELIZABETH THE QUEEN MOTHER
DONALD BROS. LTD.

## OLD GLAMIS FABRICS

DONALD BROS. LTD., OLD GLAMIS FACTORY, DUNDEE and 287 REGENT STREET, LONDON, W.1.

DESIGN 153      9

**Left:** Old Bleach showing off their royal connections, with an advertisement displaying fabrics used in the Queen's Doll's House, *Decorative Art*, 1925.

**Above:** Old Glamis advertisement with their own attempt at showing off the prestige of their wares, *Design*, 1958.

A rare use of humour in textile
advertising, *Illustrated*, 1951.

*Old Bleach*

PRESS ADVERTISEMENTS       GREAT BRITAIN   UNITED STATES

ABOVE: *Designer and Advertising Agent* : W. S. Crawford Ltd.   *Artist* : Barbara Jones, M.S.I.A.   *Advertiser* : The Old Bleach Linen Co. Ltd.
BOTTOM OPPOSITE: LEFT: *Designer*: Howard Henry. *Advertiser*: General Electric X-Ray Corporation. *Advertising Agent*: N. W. Ayer & Son Inc.   CENTRE: *Designer*:
Juke Goodman. *Artist*: Burmah Burris. *Advertiser*: Random House. *Advertising Agent*: J. R. Hanagan. *Printer*: Master Typographers. RIGHT: *Designer*: Arlosto Nardozzi.
*Artist*: Jan Balet. *Advertiser*: Nolde & Horst. *Advertising Agent*: Mabel Nolan.

56

Opposite: An atypical feminine offering for Old Bleach by Barbara Jones, 1949.

Below: Typical traditionalist inter-war advertisement, *The Ideal Home*, 1930.

of cars or cigarettes or alcohol. Foxton's 'cordially invited' people to see its products on display during the Festival of Britain and 'would appreciate a visit to our showrooms'; Grafton, advertising its ware, went as far as 'There's nothing more pleasing than Grafton Cretonnes for curtains and loose-covers'.

If furnishing fabric companies could be said to have showed off at all in their advertising it was with such items as that their wares had been chosen for this or that new building, or were being featured in a particular exhibition, or had been bought by royalty. In the 1920s, for example, The Old Bleach Linen Company made much of the fact that its linen had been chosen to deck the Queen's Doll's House; in the 1930s the Donald Bros. played on the fact that its fabrics were being used by Oliver Hill for his remarkable Art Deco Midland Hotel in Morecombe; whilst Warner's, in 1935 had advertising copy record that its wares had been selected for the Royal Academy sited 'Exhibition of British Art in Industry'. When a Royal Warrant had been issued it would appear in advertisements as in those of Sanderson's, Warner's and Old Glamis, the last frequently spelling out 'to H.M. Queen Elizabeth, the Queen Mother', rather than just featuring the warrant logo.

"Sweet Pea Bouquet" 31" wide.

This design of sweet peas against a background of soft-toned trellis makes an instant appeal to those who are, so to speak, connoisseurs of cretonne. It has a soothing beauty which makes it specially suitable for a bedroom or small sitting-room. It is a design of which one does not tire. Each pattern in the new ranges of Grafton Cretonnes has its particular charm. "Sweet Pea Bouquet" is one of the 31" range, priced at 1/11d. per yard. This range is wonderfully cheap, considering the high quality of the fabric and the beauty and variety of the patterns.

**GRAFTON CRETONNES**

There's nothing more pleasing than Grafton Cretonnes for curtains and loose-covers. We shall be pleased to send you the name of the nearest shop which sells them, or we can arrange for patterns (which are returnable) to be sent you.

THE C.P.A., LTD., 30, ST. JAMES'S BLDGS., MANCHESTER.

new
designs
in the
traditional
English
idiom

In spite of its traditional sounding name – The Old Bleach Linen Company – its advertising of its furnishing and household textiles stood out from many of the other companies by its stylish offerings in the 1930s and by its use of humour in the 1950s. A 1930s advertisement actually carried the heading 'Modern Artists design for Old Bleach', which could well have been said of the design of its advertising as for some of its textiles. As early as 1931 Old Bleach brought in the advertising agency W.S. Crawford's, run by the dynamic William Crawford, with its young art director Ashley Havinden producing some of the most original and progressive designs of the time. A Havinden design for an Old Bleach Linen booklet on 'Fabrics and Colour' featured in *Modern Publicity* in 1938 referred to the company as 'pioneers in style' when it came to press advertising. And in the 1940s the company commissioned some advertising from Barbara Jones, one a curiously feminine offering from an artist more known for thinking up concrete elephants for a Lord Mayor's Show than for sketching pale pink and blue bedrooms.

Old Bleach's use of humour in advertising its kitchen cloths was a rarity when it came to textile

*Grafton*

*Grafton*

*Grafton*

**FABRICS**

publicity. A sketch of a veiled Middle Eastern wife suggesting to her astonished husband that he use an Old Bleach pure linen Kitchen Cloth to wipe up after a dinner seems to have been one of a series issued in the early 1950s. A further one features a maid suggesting to an affronted 'lady-of-leisure' that she helps with the drying up. These were not only rare in that they used humour but also in that they were signed by the artist, not common in any advertising of the time let alone in the advertising of textiles.

When it came to the traditionalists' advertising, politeness and restraint seem to have been very much the order of the day, with a complete absence of any circus, 'Roll up! Roll up!'

**Opposite: Rosebank, traditionalists with contemporary style advertisements, *The Ambassador*, 1964.**

**Left: Grafton advertisement, *Ark*, 1965.**

MAINLY
FOR
FASHION

# The fickle world of fashion demands a constant supply of ingenious fabrics.

Roy Strong

Although some ready-to-wear clothing was marketed from the middle of the nineteenth century, when it came to women's fashions the wealthy might go to the couturiers, who were just coming onto the scene, the less wealthy to a local seamstress, but for most of the population clothes were made at home, they were long-lasting, and were adjusted or added to, here and there, as fashions changed. It was not really until the twentieth century that ready-to-wear became commonplace, and even then department stores, such as Liberty's, were still sending out catalogues from which women could order a dress or a coat in a particular colour to be made to their measurements. Still, in the early 1950s, Dickens and Jones department store employed some 130 dressmakers, tailoresses, milliners and machinists to make up customers fabric purchases.

The textile industry, or rather that part of it related to clothing, encompassed firms focusing on the various stages of production from the basic fibres, to the fabric, to the making up of actual garments. Some firms, perhaps starting with only one phase of textile production (e.g. fibres, cloth, finishing products or clothes) developed to combine more

# Horrockses
*Fashions*

**IF ONLY SHE'D KNOWN BEFORE**

There's absolutely no need to wear frocks that crease so easily. You can have dresses for every hour of the day in Tootal crease-resisting fabrics, which crush as little as costly silks and wools. And how little they cost in comparison! Why you can have two or three gowns now for the price of a single expensive satin! Don't be afraid to launder them either. They wash like silk itself—staunch to their charming colours and patterns—true to their power to resist the tiresome crease. They are sold by the brand names given below. Each carries the Tootal Guarantee of satisfaction and has its own brand name on the selvedge. If any difficulty write Tootal (Dept. 00), 56 Oxford Street, Manchester.

**TOOTAL CREASE-RESISTING FABRICS**

**ROBIA** cotton voiles    **TOOTAL FOULARD** 100% rayon    **TOOTRESS** rayon and cotton

**TOOTAL CHIFFON** 100% rayon    **TOUTALINE** cotton tweeds    **TOOTAL TAFFETA** 100% rayon.

Left: Flannel morphed into fashion, Horrockses, *Vogue*, 1953.

Above: Tootal press advertisement, *Modern Publicity*, 1934–35.

than one of these phases, making for example, both the fabric and from it the finished garment. Typical of these were Tootal, Horrockses, William Hollins's Viyella and Cresta.

The first three of these were originally businesses based on cotton, but each developed its own particular yarns that became their selling points. Tootal with its crease-resisting products, Horrockses with its own version of twisting and mixing, and Hollins's with its mixing of cotton and wool. All three went on to develop and sell cloth, Tootal and Horrockses for household linens as well as for clothes, Hollins, a later starter, moving from its yarns for the hosiery trade to Viyella, which it claimed to be the first branded fabric in the world.

By the turn of the century all three were making clothing, initially largely concentrating on underwear, nightwear, shirts and blouses. It was not really until the 1940s that they became significant players in the 'fashion' world, Tootal selling dress fabrics, Horrockses cotton, adopted by the New Look, launching Horrockses Fashion in 1946 (much favoured by the Queen and the princesses), and Viyella, by that time a major brand worldwide,

licensing its name to fashion houses making up from its fabrics.

Tootal, with its 'crease-resistant' sales line, had its advertising agency in the 1930s (Paul E. Derrick) give it a classy image, with men in dress suits accompanying women in evening dresses. Into the 1950s its sophisticated women in dresses of Tootal printed cotton were featured in its advertisements going to luncheon parties or an 'afternoon affair', whatever that was! For its children's line (Tobralco) the children, portrayed in its advertising, were clothed in Christopher Robin type gear, partying in quite clearly Georgian houses or smartly attired in private school uniforms. Yet in spite of its attempt to go up-market with quality implied, Tootal advertisements curiously nearly always carried a guarantee which may have made a potential buyer falter:

> Should dissatisfaction arise through any defect Tootal will replace it or refund the price and pay the cost incurred in making up.

Horrockses, as Tootal, continuing to produce household textiles whilst establishing its footing in the fashion world, in the post-war years had

HERE'S the very thing for a luncheon party or an afternoon affair, you say. But there's no need to restrict it to such occasions. It's made of Tootress, which isn't nearly as expensive as it looks and is quite practical everyday wear. Tootress is one of the now famous Tootal range of crease-resisting fabrics. It resists and recovers from creasing just as the best silks do. Wash as silk and it keeps its crease-resistance. Plain and patterned, Tootress offers a wonderful variety of styles and colours. It's 36 inches wide, and the name is on the selvedge for easy identification. Every yard carries the Tootal Guarantee:

"Should dissatisfaction arise through any defect whatsoever in the material, Tootals will replace it or refund the price and pay the cost incurred in making-up."

*Cuttings to demonstrate the crease-resisting power of the cloth will be sent on request. Ready-made frocks in Tootress are available, including that illustrated, No. L153.*

★

THE TOOTAL RANGE OF
CREASE-RESISTING FABRICS INCLUDES:
**TOOTRESS** RAYON AND COTTON
**TOOTAL LINEN**
**NOBIA** A BEAUTIFUL NEW STYLE OF COTTON
**TOOTAL GEORGETTE** ALL-RAYON PRINTS
**TOOTAL CHIFFON** ALL-RAYON PRINTS
**TOOTAL TAFFETA** ALL-RAYON PRINTS
**LOVA** RAYON AND COTTON

★

TOOTAL BROADHURST LEE COMPANY LIMITED (DEPT. T) 26 56 OXFORD STREET, MANCHESTER

## Ladies in waiting—

All eager to see the show. And what a picture they themselves make in their gay Tobralco frocks. Quite a part of the decorations. And long after the rejoicings are over they'll continue to look decorative. For Tobralco is one of those permanently pleasant and cheerful things we may enjoy every day. In it the children always look their best——yet it's not too precious for everyday wear——even for knockabout frocks. Nothing stands up to hard wear and repeated washing like Tobralco. Nothing keeps its colour so well, or has such wealth of colours and patterns to choose from. See the many lovely designs in the children's range——gay pictorial, ABC, nursery rhyme and floral patterns. All guaranteed, for Tobralco is a Tootal fabric.

# TOBRALCO
### SO EASY TO WASH – SO HARD TO WEAR OUT
Now only 1/6 a yard. 36 inches wide. Name on selvedge.
TOOTAL BROADHURST LEE COMPANY LIMITED (DEPT. 44) 56 OXFORD STREET, MANCHESTER 1

**Above:** Tootal advertisement listing their range of fabrics, *Woman's Journal*, 1935.

**Right:** Tootal's childrens fabric Tobralco, *Woman's Journal*, 1937.

Alastair Morton of Edinburgh Weavers designing for it, resulting not only in attractive designs but striking advertising to sell them. From the 1930s Horrockses had not been particular backward in its advertising with its tag 'the greatest name in cotton'; and its confidence grew to such an extent that eventually Horrockses Fashions felt able, in its advertisements, merely to have a photo of a model in a Horrockses' dress along with the company's name, occasionally even venturing a sexual innuendo 'men really go for a Horrockses dress'.

But it was William Hollins with its Viyella brand which really understood the importance of advertising from the start. Although Viyella was originally considered a mere sideline to supplement the firm's yarn making for the hosiery trade, by the end of the nineteenth century it had become nearly half of the company's output and, in 1910, Hollins decided to become further integrated when it set up its own garment factory. It not only relied for sales by having a brand name and by its salesmen selling directly to retail outlets, but had, at its head office in Nottingham, Viyella House, its own advertising department. Its staff proved to be innovative not only with press advertising but with

Tootal advertisement for 'Tootress' rayon, their dress material, *Milady*, 1957.

FASHION'S FAVOURITE **FABRICS**

**come to town**

Go to your favourite shop and examine Horrockses wonderful materials — for your dresses, for your lingerie, for your children. See their enchanting new designs, feel their exquisite texture. Think what charming things you could make with these wonderfully inexpensive materials. There is a Horrockses fabric for every need — and for every pocket.

HORROCKSES IN THE HOME

Sheets, pillow-cases, bedspreads and towels — in the most fashionable styles. Remember, Horrockses fabrics have been famous for every household purpose for over a hundred years.

# HORROCKSES

Horrockses publicity by Hans Schleger, 1935.

point-of-sale advertising, shop displays and display weeks in stores.

When it came to press advertising Viyella not only took spaces in the national press but in local newspapers, where it included names of local shops where Viyella could be purchased. Concerned to expand its exports, it advertised abroad, as in the American press where it made the most of such corniness as 'Vi-ella rhymes with hi-fella' and put out such nonsense as:

> Viyella is made by an English firm called William Hollins, who have been in business, man and boy, since 1784. Their mills are on the edge of Sherwood Forest, the home of Robin Hood.

Viyella advertising carried images of 'men about town' types, even when portraying them in pyjamas; whilst mothers were of the leisure ilk with indulgent nannies for their children; Hollins had developed its own children's line, Dayella, since the turn of the century. In 1966 *The Journal of Advertising Media* was to write about Viyella's advertising of its children's clothes:

**Below:** Advertisement for Horrockses children's wear, *Vogue*, 1952.

**Right:** Combined brand advertisement publicising Horrockses at Cresta, undated.

*RIGHT from the start . . .*

these lovely gay and smartly cut children's frocks have been a great success. They are simply delightful — the children just adore them.

**Horrockses**

*Pirouette*

**CHILDREN'S WEAR**

# Horrockses REGD

*at* CRESTA

EXCLUSIVE TO CRESTA and with that Special Touch of Horrockses are the fine printed cotton which buttons through in backgrounds of turquoise, magenta-red, slate grey, blue-grey, ink-blue and lilac at

**£4.9.6**

and the superfine poplin which buttons to just below the waist in black, navy, yellow, beige, light grey, slate, red and royal at

**£5.9.6**

Do visit the Horrockses floor at CRESTA 174 Regent Street or see the astonishing selection at your local CRESTA shop

POST ORDERS ACCEPTED at 174 Regent St. W.1 (please add 2/- to your cheque for postage and packing and state second choice of colour).
Hip sizes 34" to 44"

**CRESTA**
174 REGENT STREET,
NEW BOND STREET, BAKER STREET,
BROMPTON ROAD, SLOANE STREET,
WELWYN GARDEN CITY,
BRISTOL, BATH, BRIGHTON,
BOURNEMOUTH, CAMBRIDGE,
FOLKESTONE, FALMOUTH,
PENZANCE, ST. IVES.

men really

GO

for a

**Horrockses**

dress

Style No.G338
in printed poplin
Sizes: 12-18.   Price: 6½ gns.

The copy and the shot, each in their own way, enter the fantasy world of children, but since they were Viyella children naturally their world is one of almost Edwardian security, where all the afternoons are golden walks in the park, and where red-coated guardsmen played nursery rhymes on golden trumpets, and golden-hearted nannies pirouetted among the rhododendrons.

The balance between direct selling by sales people and press advertising is well illustrated in the marketing of Viyella and its cheaper line Clydella. Initially Hollins had focused on having salesmen on the road, with the result that by the turn of the century some two thousand retail outlets were carrying Hollins's products and a London office had been set up. But then advertising took precedence and much of Viyella's success was related to this. Come the depression of the early 1930s, with an accumulation of unsold out-of-fashion stock and rising manufacturing costs, Hollins cut its advertising budget and returned to old-established direct selling, increasing its sales staff from thirty to one hundred. Yet both proved to be necessary – sales staff needed the

## FASHION'S *FINEST* FLANNEL

... 'Viyella'... is guaranteed unconditionally to wash without shrinking, stretching or fading. No other flannel is like this! And because Nicolls have tailored it ... just as they'd tailor a suit or coat ... you will feel as poised in a dress this summer as you would in your best tailor-made ... but you'll look cooler, gayer and more summery American sizes '2 to 20.

**70/-**

*Send to the nearest listed shop for a folder showing 12 styles in colour.*

H. J. NICOLL & CO. LTD.,
45 WARWICK ST.,
LONDON,
W.I.

### get yours at —

ABERDEEN : John Falconer & Co. Ltd.
BATH : Jolly & Son Ltd.
BEDFORD : E. P. Rose & Son Ltd.
BIRKENHEAD : Robb Bros. Ltd.
BIRMINGHAM : Rackhams
BRISTOL : Jolly & Son Ltd.
BURY ST. EDMUNDS :
    Plumpton & Sons Ltd.
CAMBRIDGE :
    W. Eaden Lilley & Co. Ltd.
CANTERBURY : Martins Ltd.
CARLISLE : Samuel Jesper Ltd.
DERBY : Barlow Taylor & Co. Ltd.
DUNDEE : Draffens
EASTBOURNE : Bobby & Co. Ltd.
EXMOUTH : Louvil, The Strand
GLASGOW : Daly & Sons Ltd.
GREAT YARMOUTH : Palmers
HARROGATE : McDonalds Ltd.
HASTINGS : White & Norton Ltd.
HUDDERSFIELD :
    Brett, 26 John William St.
IPSWICH : A. J. Ridley & Son Ltd.
LANCASTER :
    C. E. Barrow, 10 New St.
MANCHESTER : Finnigans Ltd.
NORTHAMPTON : Adnitt Bros.
NORWICH : Chamberlins
NOTTINGHAM :
    Griffin & Spalding Ltd.
OXFORD : Elliston & Cavell Ltd.
ST. ALBANS : W. S. Green Ltd.
SHEFFIELD : T.B.& W. Cockayne Ltd.
SOUTHPORT : Boothroyds Ltd.
SUTTON :
    Mary Dunand Ltd., 6 The Pavement
TUNBRIDGE WELLS : Mary Lee Ltd.
YORK : Leak & Thorp Ltd.
**LONDON** : Nicolls of Regent St.

Left: Combined advertisement for Viyella and Nicoll, *Vogue*, 1939.

Above: Viyella wartime publicity for service shirts, 'The Shirt – for the man – for the job', 1941.

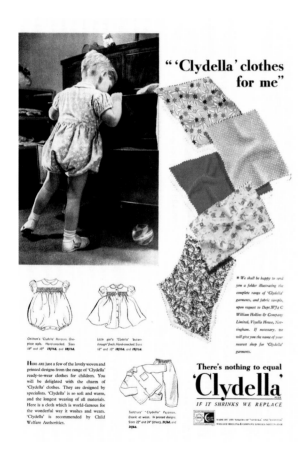

priming of advanced advertising, advertising needed sales people to follow it up.

Hollins had shown little interest in the developing synthetic fibre scene and with the limited seasonal output of Viyella it being a mixture of cotton and wool, and ineffective management at the time, the company became vulnerable. Like a cuckoo in the nest, when Hollins did eventually consider synthetics merging its business with Joe Hyman's Gainsborough Cornard, Joe, 'a man of conspicuous business ability and vision' soon cut his way through to become Chairman of Hollins. Viyella, which had been a subsidiary, came to swallow up the parent company, which Joe proceeded to build into Viyella International – a multi-fibre, multi-process fully integrated textile group. Hollins had morphed from a modest firm selling yarn to the hosiery trade into an international fashion brand. If its advertising had been strong, full-paged, coloured and proud before Hyman's arrival, it was, from 1961, able to carry the tag 'the world's best-bred fabric'.

Above: Viyella publicity at its most confident,
*The Ambassador*, 1961.

Right: Tootal targets the youth market with
fashion fabrics, *The Ambassador*, 1961.

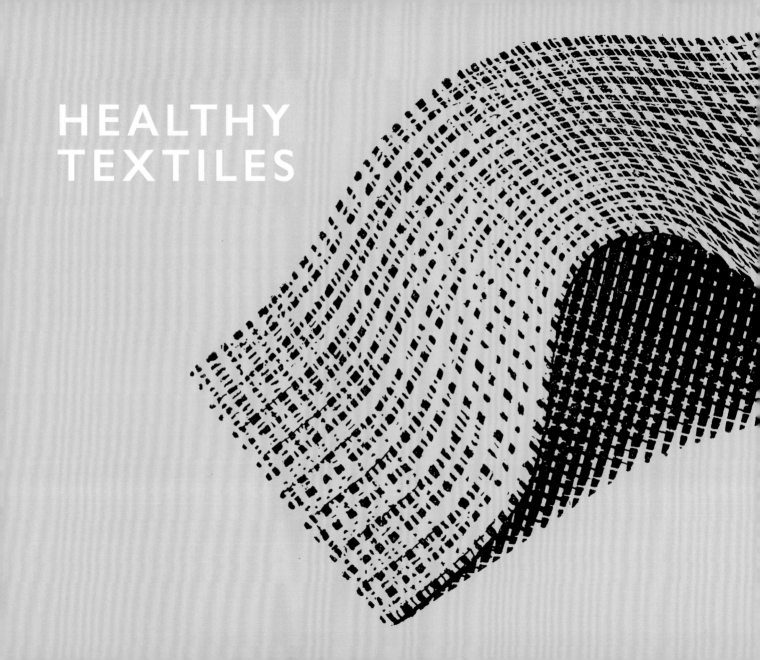

# HEALTHY
# TEXTILES

A new gospel has reached us ... it is a medical
theory, based on the close observations of animal
life, demonstrated by scientific experiment and
proved by practical experience.

*The Times*, 1884

*he Times* was reporting the arrival of Jaeger.
Linking different textiles to health can be
traced back to classical times when the
progress of the body odours through to the outside
was thought to be hindered or helped by what was
being worn next to the skin. Over time arguments
were made for or against various fibres and their
reaction to body physiology and climatic conditions,
bringing alongside such eccentricities as electric and
magnetic garments hyped for curing rheumatism
and being good for the bowels.

But Jaeger was one of the first branded textiles
relating to health that made a serious and sustained
impact on the market. One, Lewis Tomalin, actually

# CHILPRUFE for CHILDREN

WHEN one thinks of Chilprufe, one thinks not so much of the Delightful Fabric and Beautiful Garments, but of the Wonderful Protection it affords against the insidious Climate of our English Winter.

The further Reduction of Price this year makes Chilprufe better value than ever.

There is also a wide range of Chilprufe under-garments for Ladies.

*Ask your Draper, or write direct for a copy of the*

## NEW ILLUSTRATED PRICE LIST.

*If unable to obtain Chilprufe, write, addressed to the firm, for name of nearest Agent.*

THE CHILPRUFE MANUFACTURING CO.
(JOHN A. BOLTON, M.I.H., Proprietor), LEICESTER.

Chilprufe for children publicity,
*Ideal Home,* 1927.

a wholesale grocer at the time, happened upon a text by a German, Gustave Jaeger. This was a complex theory of hygienic dress, the nub of which was that wearing wool next to the skin encouraged perspiration which was good, whereas wearing vegetable fibres or silk was 'positively injurious to health' – chilling the skin too quickly which would then become saturated with perspiration. Wool would insulate the body against heat loss and shield the body against excessive heat gain. This line chimed in with the Campaign for Rational Dress which had been operating in England from 1881, further publicized by a major health exhibition held in 1884.

Tomalin quickly obtained rights from Jaeger and opened the first Jaeger shop in the City of London in 1884. The 'wool' theory was adopted by the intelligentsia, with Oscar Wilde escorting ladies to the shop expounding on the theory that wool was best; whilst Bernard Shaw, friendly through shared political views with one Andreas Scheu, who happened to be a Jaeger agent, was to be found walking along Oxford Street in a 'onesie', a kind of woolen baby grow for adults. From then on, Shaw, in spite of his commitment to vegetarianism, would besport a brown woolen suit.

# back to school—with
# JAEGER

**N**EW Clothes are wanted for the new term, and the best of all is Jaeger. It is pure wool (Nature's own clothing), and therefore the ideal wear for the health of your young people.

There are Underwear, Hose, Knitted Wear, Dressing-Gowns, Coats, Flannel Suits, Gym. Frocks, etc., in wonderful ranges at the Jaeger Shops and Agents in every town.

*Jaeger Underwear is replaced if it shrinks.*

## JAEGER
*Pure Wool*

*London Retail Branches:*
352-354 Oxford Street, W.1 ; 85-86 Cheapside, E.C.2 ;
102 Kensington High St., W.8 ; 16 Old Bond St., W.1 ;
26 Sloane Street, S.W.1 ; 131A Victoria Street, S.W.1 ;
456 Strand, W.C.2.

Jaeger publicising wool for healthy youngsters, *Punch*, 1929.

81

For something utterly flauntworthy—The JAEGER Fashion Floor, Oxford Street.

JAEGER

Only the lambiest lambs supply the JAEGER Fashion Floor, Oxford St.

JAEGER

All the most amusing people shop on The JAEGER Fashion Floor, Oxford St.

JAEGER

COATS FROM benign and natural camels — at the JAEGER fashion floor, Oxford Street

JAEGER

For really spirit-lifting GARMENTS JAEGER fashion floor, OXFORD ST.

JAEGER

Travels of elysian elegance START at the JAEGER fashion floor, OXFORD STREET

JAEGER

Jaeger's early advertising not only appeared in the national press but in such specialist publications as *The Sanitary World* and *The Cycling Times*. But Jaeger, as other textile firms, also made use of architectural swagger, when in 1902, it established its first shop in Edinburgh, of such significance as to be visited by an Architect's Congress being held in the City at that time. And Jaeger, in its advertising, was to exploit the fact that its wool-based clothing was used by such intrepid explorers as Shackleton and Scott. Jaeger, as manufacturer, wholesaler and retailer, did not have to rely on press advertisements as much as other textile manufacturers, but

nevertheless, in what advertising it did release it continued to stress its health connection through the 1930s as in a *Punch* advertisement for school clothing:

> It is pure wool (Nature's own clothing), and therefore the ideal wear for the health of your young people.

Although further generations of Tomalin carried on at Jaeger it began to reduce its 'hygienic' connections, building itself up into a major up-market fashion brand. By the mid-thirties it was using a

smart new advertising agency – Colman, Prentis &
Varley (CPV) – with its advertisements illustrated by
Terence and Betty Prentis, and later by the major
fashion illustrator Francis Marshall; not a whiff of
the healthiness of their products was to be found,
albeit the brand was to retain something of its
sportive image.

Wolsey, as Jaeger, was to move its focus from
health to fashion. The company had been manufacturing textiles in Leicester, under one name or
another, from 1755, but only became Wolsey in 1920
(named for the sole reason that Cardinal Wolsey had
been buried in Leicester Abbey). Although trading
directly with retailers Wolsey, nevertheless, became
a major advertiser, both nationally and internationally. Largely know for its hosiery it expanded its
range to include both men and women's underwear,
with occasional sallies into knitwear and swimwear.
Like Jaeger its early advertising concentrated on
the health giving aspects of wearing wool with the
caption 'Wear Wolsey and be Well'. An early advertisement played on the recency of WWI:

The health protective value of wool next-
to-the-skin is unequalled. It is your sweet

Opposite: A series of advertisements for Jaeger
by Betty Prentice of W.S. Crawford, 1931.

Above: Wool becomes fashionable, Francis Marshall
drawing for CPV, 1952.

# Wear Wolsey and be well.

Why Wolsey? Because Wolsey is PURE WOOL, the cleanest, and the softest wool — the best health safeguard in the world.

Why the finest health safeguard? Because no one has yet discovered or devised anything to equal pure wool for keeping the body's temperature equable under swiftly varying conditions of heat or cold, and only by keeping the body's temperature equable can you maintain health. Good for those who are strong, Wolsey is priceless for the weak—it is a veritable 'constitution' in itself. You can

## WEAR
# WOLSEY
## AND BE WELL

If you have any difficulty in seeing the full range of Wolsey garments, we shall be pleased to send you the name of the nearest retailer, who will gladly render you the service to which you are entitled.

WOLSEY · LTD · LEICESTER

C.F.H. 11.

Wolsey focused on health,
*The Ideal Home*, 1931.

safeguard against countless ills… Our soldiers were clad in wool, and throughout unparalleled weather conditions, it maintained the Army's health at an unusually high standard.

A slightly more explanatory advertisement appeared in *Ideal Home* in 1927:

…no one has yet discovered anything to equal pure wool for keeping the body's temperature more equable under swiftly varying conditions of heat or cold, and only by keeping the body's temperature equable can you maintain health. Good for those who are strong, Wolsey is priceless for the weak – it is a veritable 'constitution' in itself.

The linkage of wearing wool to healthiness was played upon when John Bolton, a doctor's son, living in Leicester, set up a children's garment factory in 1906, the Chilprufe Manufacturing Co. Bolton, himself, had risen through the textile trade to become a finishing manager initially setting himself up in business with The Blanket Dye Works. In

Mesdames! M'messieurs
Great indeed is your prob-
lem, but not so much as you
think! True, the new frocks
for this winter call for a great
English slenderness! But, you
English, you have answered yourselves. Your Wolsey One-piece is
quite what Paquin, Chantal and
Lelong have said should be worn
beneath these so slender gowns and
costumes, yes. The single slim-fitting
garment. Chic! Slender! But cosy
too. Paris has made for you the perfect
fashions. Yourselves, you have made the
perfect underwear. Vive!

*In wool or wool-and-silk. Prices from 8/11*
*Slender, Women's or Outsize.*

the slendered
**WOLSEY**
one-piece

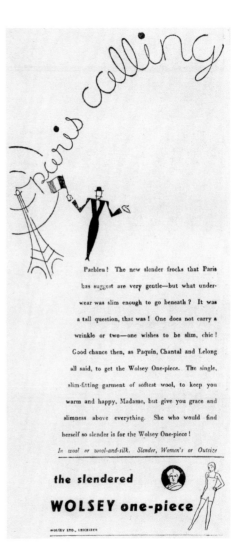

Parbleu! The new slender frocks that Paris
has suggest are very gentle—but what underwear was slim enough to go beneath? It was
a tall question, that was! One does not carry a
wrinkle or two—one wishes to be slim, chic!
Good chance then, as Paquin, Chantal and Lelong
all said, to get the Wolsey One-piece. The single,
slim-fitting garment of softest wool, to keep you
warm and happy, Madame, but give you grace and
slimness above everything. She who would find
herself so slender is for the Wolsey One-piece!

*In wool or wool-and-silk. Slender, Women's or Outsize*

the slendered
**WOLSEY** one-piece

Above and right: Two advertisements for Wolsey
showing their move from health to fashion, by Pritchard,
Wood & Partners, 1933.

85

Chilprufe, *The Strand*, 1933.

Chilprufe goes fashionable, *Ideal Home*, 1966.

diversifying into children's clothing it was wool that he made its main selling point, the link to health encapsulated in the name 'chill' and 'proof'. Early advertising spelt this out:

> ...protects children completely from all chills and sickness resultant from temperature and weather changes – and from the danger of overheating.

The precise mechanism his clothes offered seems never to have been spelt out exactly, yet repeatedly referred to in a variety of ways in its advertisements. In one appearing in the masculine focused *Strand Magazine*, in 1931, it was suggested that Chilprufe 'absorbs the moisture of the body without becoming clammy'. And in an advertisement for Chilprufe for Ladies in an *Ideal Home* from the same year it was described as essential 'when strenuous exercise means overheating and dangerous cooling down'.

Although Chilprufe's production was cut back throughout WWII, it was allowed to continue with its cheaper ranges put out under different brand names as Lainder and Narcissus. The company maintained its health links after the war as in an advertisement in the 1950s: 'Chilprufe's finest wool is a sure protection against colds and chills.' But as with Jaeger, a more fashionable note crept into Chilprufe's advertising and it began using cotton or a cotton and wool mix, diluting its message. Eventually the children's market was to be swamped by low-cost foreign imports and by British children's clothes competitors as Ladybird, whose owners, Coats Viyella, were eventually to buy up Chilprufe.

Although the advertising of woolen textiles generally came to drop the specific link to colds and other such ailments, occasionally it would pop up again in the advertising put out by the International Wool Secretariat, as in an *Ideal Home* advertisement of 1946:

> Take it from me WOOL is the healthiest for children's play... You can't tell children not to get overheated. They do! Let lightweight wool protect them naturally from damp and chills...

It was Aertex that took up the cause of wool's rival, when it came to health – cotton. The benefits were

# AERTEX
## Cellular Clothing

*Clothed with Air*

THE man who says that tennis is too energetic doesn't know the glorious feeling of cool wearing qualities of Aertex. Comfortable, hygienic and "safe" underwear is essential to all sports enthusiasts —and when we say safe we mean in its protection against quick climatic changes.

Aertex provides this safety by maintaining a layer of even temperature air next the body.

*ILLUSTRATED PRICE LIST*

of full range of Aertex Cellular Goods for men, women and children, with list of 1,500 Depots where these goods may be obtained, sent post free on application to The Cellular Clothing Co., Ltd., Fore Street, London, E.C.2. A selection from List of Depots where Aertex Cellular Goods may be obtained— LONDON—R. Scott, 8, Poultry, Cheapside, E.C.2 ; Oliver Bros., 417, Oxford Street, W.1. BIRMINGHAM—Hyam & Co., New St. BRIGHTON —F. W. Yeomans, Western Road, Hove. CAMBRIDGE—Joshua Taylor & Co., Ltd., Sidney Street. CARDIFF—E. Roberts, Ltd., 30, Duke Street. DONCASTER—A. Gamman, 24, High Street. EDINBURGH—Stark Bros., 9, South Bridge. GLASGOW—E. Jackson, 100, Buchanan Street. ILFRA-COMBE—J. Pugsley & Son, High Street. LEAMINGTON—Francis & Sons, Bath Street. MANCHESTER—O. W. Rickards, Old Millgate. NEW-CASTLE-ON-TYNE—Isaac Walton & Co., Ltd. NEWPORT (Mon.)— C. H. Burcham, High Street.

spelt out fairly fully in a *Picture Post* advertisement of 1939:

> To be cool when it's hot; warm when it's cold; fresh when it's muggy, you must have air next to your skin. Air is an effective insulator against temperature changes and Aertex is the only fabric that lets air in instead of keeping it out. So for all-the-year-round comfort, protection from colds and chills wear Aertex.

Aertex had been developed in 1888 and patented in 1895. As John Bolton had become enchanted with the healthiness of wool, Lewis Haslam, another textile manufacturer, in Lancashire, became interested in 'aeration'. He began experimenting with 'trapping the air within the warp and weft of fabric', as a buffer between the warmth of the skin. In fact, Haslam had initially started with wool, but soon turned to, and stayed with, cotton.

Haslam's Cellular Clothing Company's early advertising resorted to such copy as 'enables your whole body to breathe' and 'clothed in air'. Later advertising began stressing that garments made of

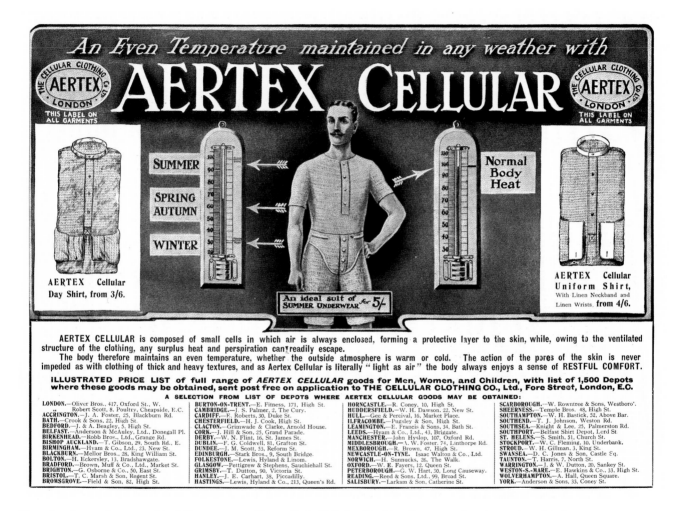

Opposite: Aertex for sport, *Ideal Home*, 1920.   Above: Early Cellular Clothing Co. press advertisement, undated.

Below: Aertex healthy the year round, *Picture Post*, 1939.

**When we invented AERTEX**

. . . we couldn't foresee a world shortage

of materials : we found that to make the

unique cellular fabric that proved warm

in winter and cool in summer, involved

a highly complicated spinning process.

So much so indeed that until restrictions are

lifted — soon we hope — the real Aertex

must remain in short supply.

CELLULAR CLOTHING COMPANY LIMITED LONDON W1

**There are many imitations but only one**

# AERTEX

Nothing is so healthful and comfortable as a cellular weave for men's and boys' underwear, for blouses for women and girls, and for corsets and pyjamas. All these garments *are* made in AERTEX, but to avoid imitations always look for the Aertex label.

*Genuine Aertex bears this label*

—and utility

**Left: Advertisement keeping the Aertex brand before the public, 1947.**

**Above: Aertex series warning of conterfeiters, *Harper's Bazaar*, 1951.**

90

Aertex had health benefits the whole year round, not just in summer:

> Aertex keeps you cool when its warm and warm when its chilly by the insulating action of millions of tiny air cells.

While 'wool' drew on the exploits of intrepid explorers to hype its healthiness, Aertex turned to sportsmen and women and their fitness. Its popularity became such that most sports teams, whether educational, amateur or professional, besported Aertex clothing, assured by the use in its advertising of such personalities as Bobby Moore, George Best and Pele. And its advertisements carried much corny jocularity as 'Aertex lowers the best handicap' (for golfers) and 'Don't let old Sol bowl you out' (for cricketers). And when war came Aertex was able to earn brownie points when it was adopted by the Women's Land Army and fitted out troops – those serving in the Far East in jungle green, those in the Middle East in khaki.

Curiously, a good deal of Aertex's post-war advertising concerned itself as much about counterfeiters as health. It had its own label for clothing, and warned potential buyers that only garments bearing that were manufactured with genuine aertex cloth. Advertising copy included 'always look for the Aertex label' and 'there are many imitations but only one Aertex' and similar cautions.

Unlike Jaeger and Chilprufe, although Aertex became a clothing company it stayed loyal to its 'health-giving' origins, much later advertising still exhorting 'wear Aertex for health'. Still, into the 1950s advertisements, as one in *Harper's Bazaar* maintained:

> Nothing is so beautiful and comfortable as a cellular weave for men's and boy's underwear, for blouses for women and girls, and for corsets and pyjamas.

TRADING
TOGETHER

RED HOT FASHION NEWS Cojana's worsted bouclé coat with exciting exit lines. Pure wool takes the credit for its rich texture and dramatic draping - the splendour of its colour. There is no substitute for wool. ® PUBLISHED BY THE INTERNATIONAL WOOL SECRETARIAT

**The International Wool Secretariat showing wool as 'Red hot fashion news', 1961.**

From the early nineteenth century when a few weavers might have banded together, or oft-times been brought together, with an agent to represent them and market their wares, elements of the textile industry have been prepared to put aside individual competitiveness to have a joint enterprise protecting them and furthering their interests.

Overtime a plethora of guilds, associations, federations, groups and secretariats, in various per-mutations and combinations, have come and gone, amalgamated and divided, sometimes based on a particular geographical area, sometimes on a particular activity within the whole process of producing fibres and fabrics, quite often based on a particular fibre or cloth being produced.

Geographically the area could be as small as one town as when Huddersfield, in 1965, produced its 'Huddersfield sells textiles' guide; or it could cover a whole country as did the Irish Linen Guild, founded in 1928, as the official promotional orga-nization for the Irish Linen industry, aiming at both national and international markets. Growing from the seventeenth and eighteenth century activities of immigrant French Huguenots and English Quakers,

Irish Linen advert with 'Irish' writ large, *Vogue*, 1939.

the Irish had become highly protective of its flax and linen products and a company could only carry the Guild's trademark if the yarn they were using had been spun in Ireland and the fabrics woven in Ireland. The Guild's promotional activities were very varied, including, post-war, the making of documentary films, but whenever it resorted to press advertising the Guild had 'Irish' written large, as in one appearing in 'The Queen' in 1953, announcing a return to the market after wartime restrictions were lifted:

> Once a woman buys Irish linen she cher-
> ishes it always for its many virtues…
> immaculate coolness for summer and
> tropical wear, glossy satin freshness of
> tablecloths and napery, purity and coolness
> of sheets and pillow cases, absorbency and
> lack of 'fluff' of kitchen and bath towels,
> the cool perfection of handkerchiefs.

A large conglomerate was the Calico Printer's association founded in Manchester in 1899, which was an amalgamation of some forty or so textile printing companies and about a dozen textile manufacturers.

Linen is in...

**IN GLASSCLOTHS** because Irish Linen glasscloths wipe drier, dry quicker, never leave fluff or linty threads and come in hundreds of colourful new designs by famous artists.

**IN TABLECLOTHS** because Irish Linen tablecloths drape gracefully, stay cleaner longer, grow lovelier with use and last a lifetime.

**IN HANDKERCHIEFS** because Irish Linen handkerchiefs are soft, smooth, more hygienic, twice as absorbent, always look clean, crisp and immaculate.

**IN PILLOWCASES** because Irish Linen pillowcases are so soft, so smooth, so warm in winter and so cool and fresh in summer.

**IN TOWELS**: In tablemats: in fabrics for furnishing and fashion : in every woven thing that means good living and makes good giving –Linen is in . . . live with Linen . . . Linen is yours for life.

*The Wonderland of Linen is always full of fresh delight . . . explore the wonder of real Irish Linen in a thousand and one colourful new designs at your nearest linen store.* (FURNITURE BY PINMAR)

*This symbol is your guarantee of real Irish Linen*

THERE'S TWICE THE LIFE IN REAL IRISH LINEN

**Irish Linen**
*Issued by The Irish Linen Guild.*

144

**Versatility of linen for households, *Ideal Home*, 1961.**

It was established:

> ...to preserve the tradition and standing of calico printing and to produce textiles of a high standard at a reasonable price.

It not only advertised its products but had progressive research laboratories, which by the 1940s, were experimenting with man-made fibres as polyethylene, later to be developed by ICI as Terylene.

Similarly the dyers of the industry had their various groupings, some just local, as the Bradford Dyers' Association, some had a national basis as the Society of Dyers and Colourists, founded as early as the 1860s.

But the largest number of promotional associations seem to have been focused on a particular fibre rather than an area or a process, as for rayon the Silk and Rayon Users Association, the Rayon and Synthetic Fibres Association and the Rayon and Synthetic Fibres Committee; whilst silk, on its own, was hyped by the Silk Association of Great Britain & Ireland. And there were similar groups for end products as well as fibres, as the Furnishing Fabric Manufacturing Association and

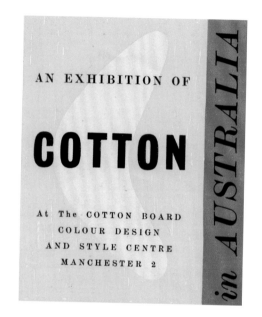

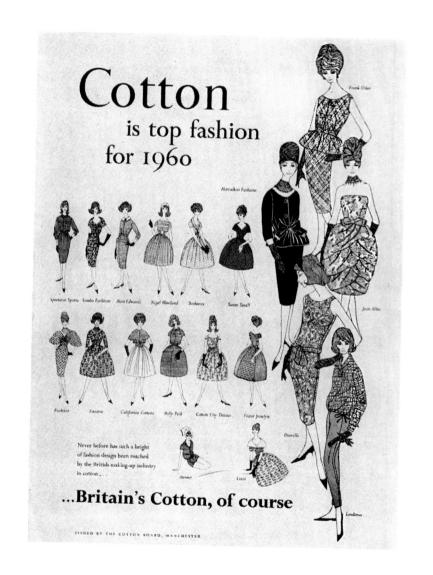

Above: Advert for one of the many exhibitions held at the Cotton Board's 'Colour Design and Style Centre' in Manchester, 1956.

Right: The Cotton Board markets fashion, S.T. Garland Advertising Services, 1960.

the Federation of Lace and Embroidery Employers Association.

Few of these had the kind of budgets that would stretch to much press advertising, but two were exceptions, The Cotton Board and the International Wool Secretariat. The Cotton Board had been set up early in the war, in 1940, initially as a voluntary body of interested parties:

> ...to promote the welfare of the industry by internal reorganization, by the development of the export trade, by scientific research, propaganda and other means.

By 1948 it had become a statutory body, part-funded by the government, part by levies on the industry. It became extremely active, show-casing cotton fabrics and fashion in cotton at national and international exhibitions, by mounting promotions in large stores, and such like. But its most innovative move was to set up in Manchester, the 'Colour, Design and Style Centre', hardly a snappy name, presumably decided by committee! This, the first British design centre, was to become the public face of the Cotton Board. Alan Peat in his book on

David Whitehead wrote of the Centre:

> Its exhibitions were to have a profound affect upon textile manufacturers and helped establish a progressive style.

The Centre's first Director was James Cleveland Belle, who had been a buyer for the Liverpool Bon Marche, and who was quickly to have the Centre make its mark. It not only put on exhibitions, but had a library, offered travelling scholarships, and set up a register of industrial art designers. Established at a totally inappropriate time, and with a lumbering name, it nevertheless had mounted some fifty exhibitions in its first decade. From the start it worked on the basis that design was the thing that would sell British textiles, mounting its first show at the Manchester Art gallery, and showing the work of art school students and members of the Textile Group of the Society of Industrial Artists. Even in its first year the Board had produced a booklet for overseas buyers which had been pronounced by Grace Lovatt Fraser as one of the most outstanding and completely successful pieces of advertising in the early war years.

*The feel of wool about the house*

FOR elegance, for homeliness, for colour and variety—for the sheer beauty of its drape and its long wear, make wool the foundation of all your furnishing schemes. On the floors, at the windows, for your cushions and upholstery, call upon the infinity of texture and the long-lasting beauty of wool to give your home that complete atmosphere of welcoming comfort.

★ *there is no substitute for* Wool

*Issued by the International Wool Secretariat*

One of the Board's most successful campaigns was 'Always Buy British Cotton', with British Cotton weeks and displays in stores throughout the Commonwealth. *Art & Industry* wrote of it:

> The fierce competition prevalent in the world's cotton markets at this time shows few signs of diminishing, and this enlightened use of advertising by the Cotton Board will obviously go a long way to ensure that when the world thinks of cotton, it thinks British first.

A Cotton Board press advertisement of 1960, considered by *Modern Publicity* to be one of the best of the year, proclaimed:

> Cotton is top for fashion for 1960... British cotton of course.

The advertisement suggesting that alongside furthering its aim for marketing the British product generally, the Board was working to raise the status of cotton specifically in the fashion industry. The advertisement named some nineteen fashion brands

Opposite: 'There is no substitute for wool', International Wool Secretariat advertisement, *Ideal Home*, 1947.

Right: 'Wool won't catch fire', advertisement from the International Wool Secretariat, *Milady*, 1952.

Below: The woolmark logo, designed by Franco Grignani, 1964.

# You can't fake the real thing.

Others put up a good case.
They talk about things like softness. Lightness.
Colour. But that's the point! They talk.
    Pure new wool is all these things.
Pure new wool. Put it on and get the feel of it.
Aaah. Cuddly. Fleecy-soft. Gentle as a caress.
    But after all, that's not surprising.
Pure new wool with the Woolmark is the real thing.
And the real thing can't be faked. No matter
how much loud talk. Pure new wool.
    Unmixed with any other fibre.
Controlled to international quality standards...
your assurance of the best.
**Look for the Woolmark label.**

**The Woolmark means Pure New Wool
the real thing.**

Wearing the Woolmark: Knockout Kilt combination.'Shetland sweater, about 4 gns. Colour co-ordinated Kilt, about 10 gns. By **MUNROSPUN.**

**Left: Advertisement featuring the highly
successful Woolmark logo, *Vogue*, 1967.**

using the fibre, including Frank Usher, Horrockses and Susan Small.

But the textile that was to be featured most frequently in the press advertising of an association was wool. Although there were a number of groups promoting wool, as the Scottish Worsted and Woolen Group and the National Wool Export Corporation, it was the International Wool Secretariat that was to flood the press in the post-WWII years.

The Secretariat had actually been established just prior to the onset of WWII when, in 1937, the wool boards of Australia, New Zealand and South Africa joined forces to promote the sale of wool in response to the onslaught of synthetic fibres. Based in London, it not only set out to sell wool, but to research and develop its usage with laboratories in Ilkley. The aim of the Secretariat was to position wool at the top of the textile market.

Its advertising covered both wool for furnishing fabrics, – 'on the floor, at the window, for your cushions and upholstery', as well as for fashion. The most familiar caption used was 'there is no substitute for wool'. But its advertising coup came in 1961 when it introduced its Woolmark logo with an accompanying advertising campaign. Initially Woolmark licensing was launched in six countries: Britain, USA, Japan, Germany, Holland and Belgium, but by the mid-'60s this had been extended to all countries with Secretariat branches.

In 1970, *The Ambassador* magazine recorded of the Woolmark advertising, both in respect of its creative quality and its commercial impact:

Advertising and communication experts in 15 countries have voted the Woolmark campaign as the most notable advertising achievement of the year in Europe.

# EPILOGUE

Textiles have their own particular challenges when it comes to advertising for it would seem essential to portray not only how it looks – its colour and patterning – but how it feels – its texture. Inevitably improvements in the advertising of textiles depended upon the development of photography. Although colour photography began to be used in advertising in the 1930s it was expensive, and it was not really until after WWII that colour advertising became rather more common, but even in these post-war years many textile manufacturers still had to rely on the imagination of the reader in looking at black and white images. The texture 'feely' quality has never been satisfactorily resolved even when some advertisers resorted to photographic close-ups which actually tended to detract from the relaying of the possible overall effect of using the fabric .

As with the development of advertising generally over the period, early textile advertisements frequently were overloaded with copy extolling the qualities of the yarn or fabric, or attempting to explain the clever technicalities of its production. As firms grew in confidence copy receded and the product was let to speak for itself. Small quarter or half page advertisements crammed with copy began to give way to full pages, the space largely filled with the attractively draped fabric. But textile advertisements would always tend to carry the firm's trademark or particular style of typographer so that the reader, attracted by the image of the fabric, would immediately be able to associate it with its manufacturer – as with Cardinal Wolsey's head, the Woolmark logo, ICI's font in its circle, or just the EW of Edinburgh Weavers.

Whatever copy was included in textile advertisements it was practically always well-mannered with few of the tricks and jokes and oftimes bullying that would become typical of such large advertisers as for cars, or drinks or cigarettes. The few attempts at devices or humour do not seem to have lasted long, and textile advertising can be said to have been largely straightforward, unemotional, and    steering clear of appealing to the consumer's basest instincts of greed or envy.

Latterly, in textile advertising of the period, there appears to have been a number of co-operative outlays between companies, particularly between fibre and fabric manufacturers, and later between fabric and garment manufacturers, and occasionally all three would be involved. Each name would be given its proportional prominence – all would share the costs and hopefully benefit from the outlay in sales.

What would have been gratifying to the descendants of the original founders of textile enterprises was the tenacity of early brand names. As minnows were swallowed by larger fish, until the textile industry became dominated by a handful of large conglomerates, such names as Tootall and

EXCITING new Tibor Textureprints, woven in high quality textured cotton, incorporating Lurex non-tarnishing metallic thread. In guaranteed fast Vat colours, they combine the beauty of colour weaving and printing. The design illustrated is called "Raw Coral." Produced by: Tibor Ltd., Stratford-on-Avon.

VICEROY deep all wool pile rug with textured effect, available in a variety of colours and sizes to your specification. In three grades, "Standard," "Super" and "Supreme." The design shown is "Broadway" by Tibor Reich, F.S.I.A. Produced by: S. J. Stockwell and Co. (Carpets) Ltd., 16 Grafton Street, London, W.1.

THE "BALMORAL" CHAIR designed by Ronald E. Long, M.S.I.A., is an example of the new range of upholstered furniture by R. S. Stevens. The outside is covered in Tibor's deep textured wool fabric "Mesh" Black / White with "Stratford" Black on the inside. Produced by: R. S. Stevens Ltd., 209 Wood Street, London, E.17.

Horrockses survived, some into the 2000s. The advertisements themselves not only mirrored the increasing role of design in marketing, particularly when it came to exporting, but reflect the integration of processes within firms and the amalgamation of firms into corporate enterprises.

Left: Tibor Reich's designs, featuring 'Raw Coral' for the hanging and 'Mesh' for the chair covering. *Design*, 1955.

# BIBLIOGRAPHY

1946 ed. Noel Carrington & Muriel Harris, *British Achievement in Design*, The Pilot Press.

1971 Jocelyn Morton, *Three generations in a family textile firm*, Routledge & Kegan Paul.

1971 Sir Ernest Goodale, *Weaving and the Warners 1870–1970*, F. Lewis Publishers.

1975 Alison Adburgham, *Liberty's: A Biography of a Shop*, George Allen & Unwin.

1981 Hester Bury, *A Choice of Design 1850–1980, Fabrics by Warner & Sons Ltd*, Warner & Sons Ltd.

1984 Susanna Goodden, *A History of Heal's: At the Sign of the Four Poster*, Heal & Son Ltd.

1984 Mary Schoeser, *Marianne Straub*, The Design Council.

1987 Valerie D. Mendes & Frances M. Hinchcliffe, *Ascher: Fabric, Art, Fashion*, V&A.

1993 Hazel Berriman, *Crysede: The unique textile design of Alec Walker*, Royal Institution of Cornwall.

1993   Jennifer Harris, *Lucienne Day: A career in design*,
       Whitworth Art Gallery.

1994   Alan Peat, *David Whitehead Ltd: Artist designed textiles 1952–1969*,
       Oldham Leisure Services.

1999   Susannah Handley, *Nylon: The manmade fashion revolution*,
       Bloomsbury.

2009   Geoffrey Rayner et al., *Jacccqueline Groag*, Antique Collectors' Club.

2009   Lesley Jackson, *Shirley Craven and Hull Traders*,
       Antique Collectors' Club.

2010   Christine Boydell, *Horrockses Fashions*, V&A.

2012   Lesley Jackson, *Alastair Morton and Edinburgh Weavers*, V&A.

2012   ed. Christopher Breward & Claire Wilcox, *The Ambassador
       Magazine*, V&A.

2014   Bramwell G. Rudd, *Courtaulds and the hosiery and knitwear
       industry*, Crucible Books.

2016   ed. Sam Reich, *Tibor Reich: Art of colour & texture*, Tibor Ltd.

Rare example of Hans Juda textile design, photograph by Rebecca Artmonsky.